A
SECRET
HISTORY

A
SECRET
HISTORY

ALISTAIR TAYLOR

Published by John Blake Publishing Ltd, 3 Bramber Court,
2 Bramber Road, London W14 9PB, England

First published in hardback in 2001

ISBN 1 903402 24 7

British Library Cataloguing-in-Publication Data: A
catalogue record for this book is available from the British
Library.

Typeset by Mac Style Ltd, Scarborough, N. Yorkshire

Printed in Great Britain by Creative Print and Design
(Wales), Ebbw Vale, Gwent

1 3 5 7 9 10 8 6 4 2

Papers used by John Blake Publishing Ltd are natural,
recyclable products made from wood grown in sustainable
forests. The manufacturing processes conform to the
environmental regulations of the country of origin.

Dedication

I would like to dedicate this book to my wife Lesley; and to the memory of Brian Epstein and all the Epstein family; and to Beatles fans everywhere. I would like to give my heartfelt thanks to Stafford Hildred, without whose help this book would never have been written.

Contents

PROLOGUE

The Beatles Anthology weighs 8 lb 12 oz and includes references to more than 2,000 people who played a part in the story of the greatest band the world will ever see. It is the Beatles' own definitive account of their momentous time together. But the man who was by the side of manager Brian Epstein when he first saw the Beatles playing, at the Cavern on 9 November 1961, is not mentioned. Apart from John Lennon, Paul McCartney, George Harrison and Pete Best, his is the only other name on the Beatles' first contract. He became the Beatles' Mr Fixit. He arranged flights, deflected paternity suits, lent money and often a shoulder to cry on. He bought islands, cars and houses for the Fab Four. He survived a determined attempt by John Lennon to turn him on to LSD. He persuaded George Harrison not to quit the group. He lost Ringo in the middle of Paris airport. And he was a grief counsellor for Paul McCartney when Jane Asher dumped him because she came home early and found him in their bed with another woman.

His name is Alistair Taylor and he has been effectively air-brushed out of official Beatles history. Yet he was the man who shared Epstein's amazing early dream of transforming this wonderful raw talent into the fabulous finished product which dazzled the globe. Today, Alistair lives on Income Support and his memories. Yet he once turned down the offer of a 2½ per cent share of the Beatles from Brian Epstein. Estimates vary, but some years ago he was reliabiliably informed that he had rejected a deal which would have given him an estimated £150 million.

In recent years Alistair has scratched a living any way he can. He has taken back-breaking labouring jobs, shovelling lead in a Dickensian factory near his tiny cottage just outside Matlock in the Derbyshire Dales and he has served as a barman and pot-washer in local pubs and hotels.

Alistair was with the Beatles from their historic first meeting with Brian Epstein through the astonishing Beatle-mania years. As a hard-working and trusted member of the exclusive inner circle, he witnessed the transformation of four young Liverpool musicians into the multi-millionaire international icons they became. Alistair was with the doctor who broke into Brian Epstein's locked bedroom door in 1967 when the charismatic manager was found dead. In the confused aftermath that followed, he was one of the loyal figures who struggled to help the Beatles reorganise their lives. John Lennon asked him to become general manager of Apple Corps and all four Beatles saw Alistair battling to bring some sanity to the commercial mayhem of that enterprise.

When the Beatles began to break apart and brash American accountant Allen Klein was brought in to take charge, Alistair was the most senior of a long list of employees who were sacked in 1969. It was a shattering blow to a man who had become totally devoted to 'the boys'. He had never fiddled a penny of his expenses, never sold a whisper of gossip and never wanted more than to play his part in the greatest entertainment success story of the twentieth century.

Yet when the axe came, he made four telephone calls – not to plead for his job, but to make sure that each of the Beatles knew exactly what was being done in their name. From John, Paul, George and Ringo, the response was precisely the same – not one of them would come to the phone. Alistair believes they were embarrassed, and having given Klein *carte blanche* to clean up the chaos they could not make any exceptions. Perhaps that embarrassment is why the name of their faithful aide does not appear anywhere in their own version of events. Who knows? Today, Alistair Taylor might be as poor as a church mouse but he is not bitter. He simply wants to tell his story.

Stafford Hildred
September, 2001

THE START

1

The advert in the Sits Vac column of the Liverpool *Echo* read, 'Young man wanted for position as sales assistant in city centre music store.' It might not look too exciting now, but at the time it promised a whole new life. The year was 1960 and I was 25 years old and stuck in a dull job as a clerk in a timber yard in Liverpool. I had worked in shops before and worked my way up as one of the bright young men of the John Lewis organisation. I'd left my home town of Runcorn for a new career in London until an accident in a supermarket damaged my spine and left me jobless.

Until then, my life had been on the up and up. In London, I shared a flat in Battersea and met the lady who is still my wife. My flatmate Nick and I used to see this gorgeous girl coming home from work every night and, in order to get to know her, we had a party. We put an invitation through her letter box and, to my delight, she accepted. We had asked her really for Nick's benefit, because I already had a girlfriend. But when she arrived, I opened the door and it was just like – *Bang* – we were instantly in love. Five days later we were engaged.

She was called Lesley, and she was gorgeous. I still think she is. We got married on Christmas Eve 1959 at Caxton Hall at nine o'clock in the morning. She had to go back to work because she managed two jewellery shops, one in Regent Street and one in Burlington Arcade. As she worked on commission, she wasn't going to take time off just before Christmas.

At four minutes past nine, we were outside on the pavement getting into a taxi that dropped her off to work. All her family thought that I had got her in the club. We had only known each other for five days when we got engaged and within a month we were married.

Life was fantastic until I slipped a disc lifting a heavy package at work. I was in agony and in plaster for eight months. I couldn't work for ages so I lost my job without any compensation. We moved back up to Liverpool where it was cheaper to live and I got a job as a clerk in a firm of timber importers. I was terribly bored. We were newly married. I was so unhappy. Lesley got fed up with me coming in every night moaning and demanded to know what would make me happy.

'I'd like to get back to retailing,' I heard myself saying. I realised that it was contact with people that I missed the most. I loved working in a shop because of the constant flow of different people who come into your life. Lesley understood. She was a sales lady. I just love the atmosphere of serving people. I started looking in the Liverpool *Echo* and, lo and behold, I saw the fateful ad: 'Young man wanted' … That was late in 1960. It concluded: 'Apply in writing to Mr Brian Epstein, NEMS Ltd., Whitechapel', so that was what I did.

I had never heard of Brian Epstein but I knew NEMS, the record shop, very well because I was a big record buyer. I was weaned on buying my first ever records there. I thought that was an incredible opportunity – to get back into selling and to move into the exciting world of music. I got a letter back asking me to come for an interview and along I went.

My interview was in the first floor office at Whitechapel where I was confronted by a very well-spoken, elegantly-dressed young man. The meeting went on for about two hours. It was great from the moment we met. We just clicked. We talked about all sorts of things. We talked about music, life, Liverpool, just about everything. Although our future was to be bound together in pop, we were both devoted to very different sorts of music. I loved jazz and Brian was passionate about classical music, particularly Mozart and Beethoven.

Our relationship was forged in that very first meeting. I knew straight away that he was 'queer', as we unkindly called it then. I wasn't. He knew I wasn't. And he knew I knew he was. And it wasn't a problem for either of us. Remember, this was at a time when homosexuality was about as socially acceptable as bear-baiting. It was a shameful and illegal practice that was widely deplored by all so-called right-thinking people. So this was quite a test for Brian to give me. Throughout our conversation, there was this subtext bubbling away under the surface.

There was a chemistry between us right from the start that is very, very hard to explain. That initial encounter turned quite quickly from being a formal interview into a discussion between friends. He could be so precise when he wanted to be. I will always remember him sitting back and saying, 'I can't pay you enough as a shop assistant', which was what the job was. 'But I have been thinking of having a personal assistant. Would you be interested?'

Of course, I said, 'Yes'. My starting salary was £10 a week and I couldn't have been more delighted. I was earning £7 10s a week at the timber yard and I was bored out of my brain there.

Before I left his office, I was even given my first job. Brian had some bullfighting posters which needed framing. Would I be so good as to take care of that?

Of course, a lot of my work was at the counter but afterwards I would stay behind and do the ordering with Brian. He had this incredible 'GOS' system, which stood for General Over Stock. NEMS became a legend for its ability to get any record at all in those days. People came from as far afield as London to see how this relatively small shop in Liverpool had built up such a fantastic reputation for serving its customers. It was so bloody simple. On every album there was a brown sleeve with a different coloured tag on. When you sold one you left the tag dangling. And at night, after the shop had closed, Brian and I would go round and, guided by the tags, order a replacement for every record we had sold.

Brian was never unwilling to supply a record. He took enormous pride in that. If a record was available anywhere in the world and people wanted to buy it, then Brian wanted to sell it. And he would get it. Even if it took him a year.

Brian was uniquely gifted. He could listen to a record along with me and I would hear nothing special and quickly write off its chances. Brian would smile quietly and say, 'All right, Alistair. Order 250.' I would be astonished.

We had two shops – the large Whitechapel base and the small Great Charlotte Street shop. But that order was always right. Brian could smell a hit record from a million miles away. We both hated pop music. I think I beat him once, maybe twice. But usually he was 100 per cent right.

When Ray Charles' version of 'Georgia on my Mind' was released, Brian was instantly impressed. 'It is sure to be number one,' he said in those elegantly modulated, carefully measured tones. I burst out laughing. I loved the song but I was convinced that never in a million years would it

9

be a hit. Brian backed his judgement with the wager of a large gin and tonic. And, sure enough, it cost me the price of his drink and taught me never to underestimate Brian's uncanny ability to predict a record's popularity.

I first heard John Leyton sing 'Johnny Remember Me' on an early television soap opera called *Compact*. We knew the record was going to be featured thanks to the enthusiasm of the rep from Top Rank and we wanted to hear it. In those days before video recorders, Brian had a dinner date which he did not want to break so I was delegated to listen and assess. I enjoyed the programme well enough but the record left me cold.

The next day, I gravely advised Brian that five copies in each shop would be more than enough. When this order was despatched to Top Rank, the rep was so disappointed he appeared in the shop with a copy of the record to see if Brian could be persuaded to change his mind. Brian and I listened together and I remained imperiously dismissive. But there was something in the lyrics that Brian liked. He asked for it to be played again and then, with just the slightest flicker of a smile, said, 'We'll take 250 copies, please.' By then, I knew much better than to protest. Brian was clearly confident that 'Johnny Remember Me' was going to be a considerable hit. I still thought it was deeply forgettable.

But Brian, of course, was right. The day it was released, we experienced an enormous rush of people wanting to listen to those haunting lyrics and it went rapidly into the charts. Our competitors on Merseyside had reacted in the same way as me and had hardly taken any copies. But thanks to Brian's ear for a hit, we had a sales rush. Brian was delighted and the rep confided that Brian's taste was rarely wrong.

Orders from NEMS were always carefully examined in the London offices of the big record companies. They knew that Brian Epstein was an expert at predicting the public reaction to a new record.

In those early days, he was not ambitious. Brian was a very easily bored kind of guy. He had done it with the furniture stores and with the record shop and suddenly something new appeared.

We became close quite soon. At 5.30pm when we closed the shop, he and I would then get together and do the ordering. And afterwards, we would go out for a gin and tonic at the Basnett Bar at the end of the day before I went home. Years later, I discovered to my surprise that the Basnett Bar was a hangout for gays. Not that they were called that then. Gay just meant happy in those innocent times.

I'd have a plate of cockles and a gin and tonic with Brian. Often, if we differed about the chances of a record becoming a hit, we would wager our usual bet of a gin and tonic. I always paid my debts and it always seemed to be me who lost the bet.

As we became more friendly, Brian would often say, 'Let's go and have dinner at the Rembrandt Club.' I loved eating there with Brian because he was such good company. We'd laugh and we'd giggle for hours. It never even crossed my mind to worry that I was sitting enjoying myself so much with a homosexual.

It annoys me that so much crap is talked about Brian nowadays. The common legend now is that Brian fell in love with John and that everything followed from that.

That's total bullshit. Excuse my French, but it's nonsense. Peter Brown's appalling book explores Brian's homosexual side in grisly detail and I'm not convinced by half of it.

Brian was always looking for some new horizon to head for. He got tired of things very quickly. Brian was an amazing man. My wife Lesley reckons that I was in love with him. And she is right. I did love him, but not in a homosexual way. The idea of going to bed with Brian, or with any man, makes me feel physically sick. It always has. But in a non-physical way, I still loved Brian. He was bright and funny and brilliant. He simply oozed charisma. Brian Epstein brightened up any room he walked into, he couldn't help it. We just hit it off straight away. There was something about Brian that inspired loyalty and devotion in me. I think he knew that. And he also knew that those qualities were not going to be found in any of the men he slept with. He kept them well away from the business.

Early on in our relationship, I remember he was going to go off to Spain. He loved the glamour and the sunshine of Spain. And he loved the spectacle of bullfighting. He insisted, 'Alistair, you must come over.' I got a cab straight over and my task when I arrived was to help him choose what clothes he was going to take with him.

He said, 'Do you think I need a dinner jacket?'

I said, 'Brian, for goodness' sake, you're going on holiday. You're going to relax, not dress up. No, of course, you don't need a dinner jacket in Spain.'

After about two days of his holiday, Brian rang me and said, 'You silly bugger. What do I need tonight? I've had to hire a dinner jacket.'

We both laughed.

Lots of people can say they slept with him and some of them have, but I honestly don't feel there was anyone closer during our time together. He could turn to me when things were rough and know he was going to get 100 per cent help.

He always wore a suit and a white shirt. He was just nine months older than me. When we first met, he somehow assumed that I was older than him and it wasn't until later that he realised. He laughed, 'I've always treated you with such respect, because I thought you were one of my elders.' It became a running joke between us.

He wasn't a hard task-master, but he wasn't easy. He could be awkward and he was a real stickler that everything had to be right. After all, he was running the best record store in the north-west of England. Then it became the north of England. Then it became the whole of England. He was the first man to stock the whole of the Blue Note jazz catalogue. Because he knew I loved jazz, he invited me to share a box at the Royal Philharmonic Hall to hear Art Blakey and Thelonius Monk.

When I first met Brian, he drove a Hillman Minx and lived at home with his mum and dad, Harry and Queenie. He and his brother Clive always called them Mummy and Daddy. They lived in a large detached house on Queen's Drive in Childwall, a very prestigious address. I went there a couple of times. Harry was a lovely, kind man. He used to come into the shop and take a look around and you could tell by his manner if there was going to be trouble, if he didn't think things were being run properly.

Brian was very inventive. When he was running the furniture store, he used to turn the furniture with its back to the shop window so shoppers could see the other side. Harry went mad, but it was unique for its time.

There was a period in the early '60s when cocktail piano music became the big thing. Brian wouldn't just put record sleeves in the window. He made a display. He would have the white cloth on the table with two glasses, two chairs and the record album sleeves. Pow, what's that? It had the desired impact, and people would stop to have a closer look.

THE MEETING
2

The story of how Brian Epstein became the Beatles' manager has now passed into Beatles legend, which sadly often means that the facts of the matter go straight out of the window. My memory is as fallible as the next man's, but I was there when it happened and, in spite of what you might have read or heard to the contrary in the avalanche of Beatles books and articles, this is the truth.

I got so fed up with people asking if we had a record of 'My Bonnie' by the Beatles and having to say No that I put through an order for it myself under a name I simply dreamed up. Brian refused to order records unless there was a firm order. Once there was an order, Brian's claim was that if the record existed, anywhere in the world, we could get it.

The famous story is that a guy called Raymond Jones came into the shop and asked for a record by the Beatles. I know that I invented the name and put it into the order book. But now Liverpool people claim to know 'the real' Raymond Jones and a chap with that name can miraculously recall placing the order. Rubbish. It was a name I picked at random because I wanted to get this bloody Beatles record that people kept asking about. But it wasn't by the Beatles.

I researched for weeks and found out that 'My Bonnie' was not by the Beatles. It was by Tony Sheridan and the backing group was called the Beat Brothers.

It turned out that the Beat Brothers were the Beatles. But we had to order it from Polydor in Germany. The minimum was 25 copies, which I ordered and had them shipped over. I bought one myself and Brian stuck his own handwritten notice up in the window saying 'Beatles Records for Sale'. And they were gone inside a couple of hours.

We played it and Brian and I both thought it was garbage, but the reaction it inspired among Liverpool record-buyers was exciting and impossible to ignore. It was a great, noisy, wonderful record. I ordered another box of 25 and they went just as quickly. We sold thousands of them and we rang Polydor and tried to tell them that something remarkable was happening here but they couldn't have been less interested. They didn't want to know about a bizarre sales flurry in an obscure provincial record shop.

But that was what kindled Brian's interest in the Beatles. Several weeks later, Brian walked into the shop and asked, 'Do you remember that record we sold by those people the Beatles? Well, they are playing over here at The Cavern. Do you know where The Cavern is?'

It was only 200 yards from where we were standing! I used to go often when it was a jazz club, in the days before the groups took over the music scene. Yet Brian was blissfully unaware of its existence. He suggested we took a look at this strangely popular group of musicians called the Beatles on our way to lunch. Brian had seen a poster advertising the Beatles 'direct from Hamburg'. People insist today that we must have known they were a Liverpool group by then. Well, maybe we should have known. But the truth is, we didn't.

One of the many Beatles myths is that Brian Epstein's arrival at The Cavern was announced by disc jockey Bob Wooller. Another is that he rang the day before and demanded VIP treatment. They are just not true. It was much more casual than that. It was almost on a whim that Brian first saw the Beatles. He was simply intrigued by this unknown group that inspired such devotion at his tills and wanted to take a quick look at them for himself. It came at a time in his life when he was bored. What inspired him to suggest we checked out the Beatles in The Cavern was curiosity, pure and simple.

It was 9 November 1961, and it took us only a few minutes to walk up Mathew Street to The Cavern. I paid at the door with two half crowns Brian had discreetly passed to me as we approached the door, which was guarded by a single, aged, snoozing bouncer. We sat right at the back. Some accounts have us nursing our briefcases. Not true. We didn't go with any intention of doing business. We were on our way to lunch.

The Cavern was a complete dump. It seemed to have gone downhill since its days as a jazz venue. There was condensation dripping down the walls. It was an old vegetable warehouse and it still stank of its former occupants. It was really hot and airless and packed with kids trying to get near the stage. The place was bursting at the seams. The girls had their beehive haircuts and the boys just tried to look cool. There was no proper bar there and Coke was the drink of the day. The noise hit you at the same time as the smell and it was hard to tell which was more upsetting.

My first reaction was 'Let's get out of here,' because on stage were four dreadful young men making the most appalling racket. They looked like typical, unpleasant youths to me. Neither Brian nor I liked pop music. It was loud. It was physical. There was so much noise you could feel the sound. And even sitting at the back, it hit us like a thump in the chest. We felt desperately out of place in our suits among all these casually dressed kids. It was an extraordinary experience. People recognised Brian and he felt increasingly uncomfortable. But we just sat there with this amazing noise and energy blasting at us.

The four Beatles were dressed in black leather jeans and bomber jackets and black T-shirts and they just looked completely out of control. I could see Brian's eyes widen with amazement as they yelled and swore at their audience between songs. They were swigging back Coke and they were smoking on stage. They were just awful. We just sat there like a pair of lemons wondering what planet we had landed on. It was one of the most shocking experiences of my life and I know Brian felt the same.

But then I suddenly found that my foot was tapping in time to the music. In spite of my job, I didn't like pop music in the least. And I certainly didn't feel drawn to this wild bunch of louts. They were the sort of lads I had always avoided at school, you know, the trouble-makers who didn't give a damn about anyone. And yet there was something earthy and undeniably attractive about them. Their confidence and their arrogance was already apparent. I just glanced round and I saw Brian's hand was tapping in time to the same rhythm. We didn't look at each other or say anything.

For 40 years since that fateful visit, I have wondered exactly what it was that Brian saw in this loud and dirty pop group. I remember saying years later to Paul that they sounded as if they only knew five chords. He replied, 'Do you mind. We only knew three.' I still don't know, but something special happened that lunchtime in The Cavern. It was mind-blowing for both of us. They were loud and they weren't very good but there was just this special ingredient. It was beyond charisma. It was beyond musicianship. It was beyond anything you could easily define.

They only played about five numbers. They sang 'Money', ''Til There Was You', 'A Taste of Honey' and 'Twist and Shout' and, in a way, they were all equally terrible. What had clinched it for me was, towards the end of their set, when Paul had said, 'We'd like to finish now with a number that John and me have written.' That was 'Hello, Little Girl', which sounded like a decent pop song to me. They never recorded it. In fact, years later they gave it to the Fourmost, another of our groups. And it became quite a big hit. Brian and I exchanged a glance. So they could write songs as well as perform them. That was pretty unusual back in those days.

The famous fable goes that Brian went to see them in their dressing room and to impress them he introduced me as his personal assistant. That's rubbish. It has been re-hashed time and time again that Brian introduced me as his PA just to dazzle the Beatles as a big-time businessman. That is simply not true. I *was* his PA. Brian was not struggling to impress the Beatles. You could see from the looks on their faces that he was already doing that quite convincingly.

We just said, 'Hello'. The so-called dressing room was a cupboard. We couldn't have all got in their dressing room if we'd tried. We recognised them because they came in the shop. We were amused that we'd thought they were some mystery German group when all the time they were Scousers. Brian said, 'I just want to say we've seen your last five songs. You were great.'

They looked a little embarrassed and thanked us and we left. In the years since, the Beatles have recalled countless wisecracks and flip remarks they made to the smooth Mr

Epstein over the years, but my memory is that the four of them were polite and extremely respectful.

We couldn't hear ourselves think and we both wanted to get out of the place and have a proper chat. Brian and I went off for lunch and I remember we hardly spoke as we left The Cavern and walked to Peacock's restaurant. They'd been so loud that I think our hearing took a little time to return to normal and we were still collecting our thoughts after a pretty shattering experience.

It took Brian less than half-an-hour to come up with the decision that was to change all our lives. He asked me what I'd thought of the Beatles and I said, 'Frankly, I thought they were awful. What a din! And yet they do have something. They look scruffy and they are not in the least professional but they do have something.'

'Yes,' said Brian, with that famous half-smile beginning to form on his handsome face. 'They are awful. But I think they are fabulous. What do you think about me managing them? I would like to know, Alistair, do you work for me or do you work for NEMS?' asked Brian.

'For you, Brian, I suppose. I'm your personal assistant,' never having considered there to be a difference. 'Why do you ask?'

'Because I am thinking about managing the Beatles and I know it will mean a lot of work and reorganisation for us. I want to know what you think of the idea. If I took on the Beatles, would you come with me? Or do you want to stay at the shop?'

It took me a moment or two to realise that he was actually serious. And I understood what he had been leading up to. I don't believe he had thought of the idea until we went into The Cavern. He was completely captivated by this remarkable raw talent that he'd seen and heard there. I believe he had an instant vision of how he could mould them into this amazing pop group that was nothing like the world had ever seen.

I was there when Brian first saw the Beatles and I don't believe for a second the endlessly repeated view that he fell hopelessly in love with John. He fell in love with the sheer energy, wicked humour and irresistible charisma of the four of them. Brian was a brilliant man who could have succeeded in any one of a hundred fields. But I think that that day in The Cavern he saw the potential of the Beatles and he was transformed by it. Straight away, he said to me that he believed they could be bigger than Elvis. It wasn't a gradual thing. There was no steady learning curve with Brian Epstein. From that day on, he just knew that he and the Beatles could conquer the world.

His enthusiasm was infectious and, of course, I wanted to be a part of his plans. He said at that lunch that he would have to set up a new management company and he invited me to join him. That sounded a whole lot more exciting than working in a record shop and I quickly told Brian that I was with him all the way. I'd love to say that I shared Brian's vision, but it would not be true. I could see that the four lads had raw talent. John Lennon and Paul McCartney might not have been the sort of boys your parents would want you playing with but there was something about their strutting arrogance and wide-eyed energy that was undeniably attractive. George Harrison was much quieter and kept in the background that day and Pete Best, the drummer, scarcely spoke at all.

But it was Brian I backed to succeed. I didn't have the remotest idea whether or not the Beatles were heading for the charts or the dole queue but I was by now convinced that Brian Epstein was going places. He simply exuded confidence and ambition. I was already in awe of Brian when we went to The Cavern. If he now had a dream to fulfil, I definitely wanted to be part of it.

Then he dropped a quiet bombshell on me. He said, 'Alistair, since you will be very closely involved with the setting up and running of this new company, I would like to give you $2\frac{1}{2}$ per cent of the Beatles' contract.'

The conversation that followed is still very painful to recall. Estimates vary but I am reasonably certain that it cost me many millions of pounds. I don't think Brian was testing me and my loyalty, but even 40 years later, when the man in question is sadly no longer around to verify it, I'm still not sure. But I said, 'Brian, I can't accept that, even though it's so generous. I have no money of my own to put into the Beatles and I know it will cost an awful lot to set the business up.'

Brian persevered, 'I don't want your money. I want your loyalty.'

But I would not be told. I said, 'You already have my complete and absolute loyalty. You will always have that. All I need is a decent salary and I'll be happy.'

With the relentless agony of hindsight, I can only think that my financial problems at the time were so pressing that a rise of a couple of pounds a week in my pay packet seemed like a much better prospect than the doubtful chances of an unwashed foursome from Merseyside taking the entertainment world by storm. How wrong can you be?

Brian let it drop. His mind was full of plans for the Beatles. Over the years, I've learned that Brian had a history of taking up projects with enormous enthusiasm and then quickly losing interest. His family and older friends thought the Beatles would just be another passing interest. I never thought that, partly because I was only just starting to get to know him well and partly because I saw a definite change in Brian Epstein that day. On the strength of listening to four undisciplined louts sing five raucous songs in a sweaty cellar, Brian Epstein was 100 per cent convinced that he had discovered the most popular entertainers of the twentieth century. And he was right.

THE CONTRACT
3

We organised a meeting in Whitechapel on a Sunday morning. We used the very long, narrow office which actually seemed more like a corridor than a room. Brian did not like to use his big office upstairs, next to the other family offices, for meeting the Beatles. Instead, he preferred the smaller office which was really an old stock room behind the shop. It was fitted with shelves which always seemed to be overflowing with record catalogues and stationery and office supplies. On the walls was a selection of Brian's favourite bullfighting posters.

Pete Best, John Lennon and George Harrison arrived and Brian was sitting up at the top end of the room with me next to him. They all sat in a line on one side.

Paul was late. We waited for about ten minutes as Brian grew very impatient and he sent George off to phone and find out where Paul had got to. George returned and said, 'He'll be here in a few minutes, Mr Epstein.'

Brian's eyebrows raised.

'Sorry, Mr Epstein,' added George helpfully. 'He's just been having a bath.'

Brian was clearly irritated by this and snorted, 'This is disgraceful. He is going to be very late.'

'Late,' said George with that guileless expression of his, '… but very clean.'

Brian didn't really get the joke. This was too important to him for jokes. He insisted that he didn't want to discuss anything to do with management unless all four of them were there.

Paul eventually arrived. The four of them were very nervous and quiet and they waited patiently for Brian to speak. He paused for a moment and I saw a couple of beads of sweat appear on his normally cool brow. I realised Brian was just as nervous as they were. This was very important to him. Slowly, he spoke. He had prepared quite a long speech which he occasionally consulted.

He believed in them and he wanted to manage them. He thought they had the ability to go right to the very top if they were prepared to put themselves in his hands. But he had never managed a group before and he knew he had a great deal to learn. He believed they had to make a great number of changes in their appearance and in their behaviour on stage if they were to realise their potential. But if they put themselves in his hands, then he believed there was no limit to what they could achieve.

They looked totally mesmerised by the experience. There was no clowning and no disrespect. I think they knew this was a very important decision they were making. They had already had their disappointments and they knew how many younger groups were coming up all the time. They had confidence in their ability certainly, but they knew that lots of people never got to fulfil their potential.

They had listened to a lot of bullshitters even then. But Brian was old enough and rich enough to be taken seriously. And he was young enough and cool enough to relate to them. John told me later that they trusted Brian from that first proper meeting.

Certainly, when Brian finished his speech and then asked them if they wanted to put their future in his hands, there was a pause. The four of them looked as if they had been brought into the headmaster's study having been caught shop-lifting. They exchanged glances and then John said emphatically, 'Yes.' He breathed out with a sort of sigh of relief, 'We would like you to manage us, Mr Epstein.'

And then the others started chiming in, 'Yes, please manage us, Mr Epstein,' 'Yes, manage us, please.'

There were several more meetings in quick succession over that hectic period. Brian also went in search of anyone who might give him advice about the task he was taking on. He learned that while no one questioned the Beatles' ability to entertain, they did not exactly have a reputation for reliability.

Another Beatles myth is that the first contract was signed at the Beatles' unofficial headquarters, the Casbah Club, run by Pete Best's mum. Again, that is untrue. Brian first produced a contract in the Whitechapel office and the four Beatles quickly signed. And I signed it as well, as a witness at Brian's request.

Then there was a strange sort of pause. I said, 'Are you going to sign, Brian?'

'Oh, witness mine as well, Alistair,' he replied. 'I'll do it later.'

But he never did. He gave the explanation later that he had not signed that original contract because he didn't want the Beatles to feel tied to him in any way. If they ever wanted to sack him, they could do so easily, without any legal difficulties. On the other hand, he said that his word was his bond and that he did not need to sign a piece of paper to prove it. This way, they could have all the benefits of being professionally managed without any of the legal obligations. I'm still not quite sure I understand his reasoning even after all these years, but I guess he more than proved his commitment to the boys. But the only five signatures on the original contract between Brian Epstein and the Beatles were those of JW Lennon, James Paul McCartney, George Harrison, RP Best and Alistair Taylor. Very strange.

There was great uproar in the office. Everyone was hugging each other and being very tactile for those days. There was lots of cheering and back-slapping. And when it all died down a bit, there was a voice from the back of the line, right at the end of the narrow little office, from the guy at the end of the row who said, 'Well, I think we're going to make it as a group. I certainly *hope* we make it as a group, but I'll tell you what – if we don't, I'm gonna be a star.' That was from Mr McCartney.

That first contract was effective from 1 February 1962 for a five-year period, but the Beatles and Brian were each able to give the other three months' notice if things went wrong. Brian was on 10 per cent of the Beatles' income up to £1,500 a year each. Once their individual earnings went over £1,500, Brian's percentage increased to 15 per cent. I don't think there has ever been anyone in the history of pop music who's had a fairer contract than the Beatles. Brian's percentage went up to 25 per cent in later contracts.

But even then they were so unbelievably lucky that Brian found them when he did. Brian set up a totally new form of management. In those days, if you were a young group then your manager or agent just said, 'Right, you're playing at Swindon tonight, Edinburgh tomorrow ...' and so on. If the members of the group had no money for petrol or hotel rooms, then that was tough and very much their problem. 'Just be there' was the instruction.

Brian set up a system which every bill they incurred came back to the office and we paid it. They always had money in their pockets, and a wage to live on. This was always deducted. We controlled all the money and managed it for them.

Brian also had a vision of how the Beatles were going to take over the world. From day one, he knew what he wanted to achieve and it was so much that at first he dared not even tell them.

Not that Brian was shy of being a hard task-master. He had a very clear idea of how he wanted the Beatles to look and behave and it was not at all like the way we had first watched them perform in The Cavern just a few weeks earlier. He pledged his determination to deliver them the recording contract which they all knew was vital to turning their regional success into national and international stardom.

And he didn't pull any punches when he told the Beatles how things were going to be in the future. Like a teacher laying down the law to his most unruly pupils, Brian said they had to stop behaving like a bunch of amateurs and transform themselves into professional musicians and entertainers.

He said, 'I want you all to make yourselves a lot smarter in appearance. On stage, there must be no drinking, no smoking, no chewing gum, and especially no swearing. The audience is not there to talk to you so don't chat to the pretty girls while you're on stage. Be punctual. If you're scheduled to arrive at a certain time, make sure you arrive when you are meant to. Remember that you are pro-fessionals now, with a reputation to keep up.'

I would hand Brian's directives to the boys and they were always neatly typed on top-quality paper with Brian's initials printed elegantly on the top. John was particularly impressed. He said, 'Brian put all our instructions down on paper and it made it all seem real. We were in a daydream 'til he came along.'

Brian was very businesslike. He knew the Beatles were in financial trouble even though they were then earning the princely sum of £3 15s each per Cavern session. This was higher than the normal rate because they were such a draw but it was an awful long way from the champagne lifestyle. Brian told them there and then that they would never play for less than £15 a night and he pledged to renegotiate their lunchtime Cavern rates. He kept that promise very quickly and they went up to £10. This was good money in 1961. Brian further impressed the shell-shocked foursome by quickly discovering the extents of their debts from a fellow shopkeeper and instantly wiped them out.

Brian found out from Bernard Michaelson, manager of Frank Hessy's music shop across the road from NEMS, that the Beatles owed an alarming £200 on various hire-purchase agreements. He paid off the debt straight away with a personal cheque which bought John Lennon the ownership of his prized Hofner Club 40 guitar, George Harrison his Futurama guitar, and paid off the remains of Paul McCartney's payments on amplifiers. It was a simple but stunningly convincing act that instantly established a bond between Brian and the Beatles.

Brian spelled out to the Beatles that they must look the part as well as act it, and took them over to Birkenhead to a tailor to be measured for their new suits. The mohair suits cost £40 each, which Brian paid, of course. I can well remember the wide-eyed acceptance that greeted that

particular instruction. Subsequently, the Beatles have suggested that they did not totally go along with Brian on
wearing suits. John sneered years later that he felt that he
was selling out. My memories of the Beatles' reaction is
rather different. They were so fed up of failing to get
noticed and failing to make it to the top that if Brian had
said he wanted them to climb to the top of the Liver Building and jump down into a bucket of custard they would
have said, 'Where's the bucket?' It didn't take them long to
realise that Brian was right, and that he knew what he was
doing.

Brian *never* tried to interfere with their music. It was all
to do with their presentation, their behaviour and their
image. Brian embarked on a total clean-up job on the four
boys. Haircuts followed the suits and complete new
wardrobes of shirts, ties, shoes, everything followed. Brian
asked them face-to-face if they had any objections to his
plans and there wasn't even a murmur of dissent. Just as
Brian believed in the Beatles, it was clear from the very start
that the Beatles believed in Brian.

We took the famous ferry across the Mersey and Brian
and I must have looked like a couple of plain-clothes policemen escorting four dangerous criminals. Brian and I got to
know the four of them a little better. With the business of
the contract out of the way, we were all on the same side
now. John was clearly the strongest character among them,
but the four of them seemed to communicate in a language
almost of their own which was bound up with jokes,
sarcasm and the blackest of humour. But, gradually, as the
ferry made its way across, I even began to understand a little
of what they were talking about.

I realised that just because they looked scruffy and aimless they were not to be dismissed easily. When we disembarked, we had a 15-minute walk to Brian's tailor and the boys were all excited at the thought of getting their first made-to-measure suits. Brian went straight into a huddle with Beno Dorn, the little Jewish tailor who was clearly an old friend. The boys gazed open-mouthed at the up-market establishment. I think their experience of tailoring up until then was a quick glance in Burton's window. Brian quickly had it all sorted out. The boys were to be kitted out in smart, dark-blue suits, a very different look from their usual black leather.

It was a great day out as the boys enjoyed being the centre of attention. The only downside to the day came when we got back to the shop and Brian discovered that none of the record companies he had contacted had called him back. Clearly, selling a new group to the record companies was going to be quite different from selling records to the public.

The following day it was haircuts and the beginning of the creation of the famous mop tops. Brian and I took the boys to Horne Brothers who then had a reputation as very classy hairdressers. Their long hair was trimmed and styled into a much more clean-cut image. They were becoming just the sort of boys every girl would soon be screaming her head off for. Much to their relief, the hair was still left reasonably long but the greasy untamed look was definitely a thing of the past. John grinned that his Aunt Mimi would think he had turned over a completely new leaf: 'It seems almost a shame to give her too many false hopes.'

The haircuts were followed by a morning in Liverpool's top men's outfitters and they returned each proudly clutching parcels of new clothes. They were like kids at Christmas as they rushed to open their new presents. Each of them had bright new shirts and ties, which were certainly a novelty and took some getting used to. Everything was carefully selected with Brian's eye for style and colour. I think he enjoyed the shopping trip more than any of us.

This was a special time to be around the Beatles. They were bright and funny and so full of life you wished you could bottle their energy. I'm not saying they knew they were going to make it, but there was a kind of inner confidence about them that you could never quite put your finger on. For them, something of the pressure of getting the success they all craved had slipped on to Brian's shoulders so they seemed to relax under the new Epstein regime.

THE RECORD
4

The Beatles were still very respectful and polite but there was a real friendship building here. But they were proud northern lads and there were moments when they wanted to discuss things with their sophisticated new manager man to man. I remember one night in the Tower Ballroom, New Brighton, when the six of us were having a drink. Brian had been to the bar and I had bought the second round. Suddenly, I felt a tap on the knee under the table. It was John indicating to me that he was embarrassed to find that he hadn't the price of a round on him and yet he anxiously wanted to stand his round. I slipped him a £1 note under the table and instantly heard John grandly asking Brian if he felt like another.

My main job in the next few weeks was covering up for Brian. He would be holed up in Brown's Hotel in London on a desperate round of calling in every record company contact he had, just to clinch the all-important first recording contract. He just pounded the pavement, determined to get someone to listen.

Brian was a big noise in Liverpool, but he wasn't so important down in London. It took a lot of time and it took him away from the shop. Harry would come in two or three times a week in search of Brian, who naturally neglected to tell his father that he was going to be down in London trying to get a start for the Beatles.

As it turned out, signing the Beatles was the easy bit. Getting a record company interested was much more difficult. There were more than 300 rock groups in Liverpool in the early 1960s. All of them wanted a recording contract.

In those days their work-rate was absolutely amazing. They did so many gigs that when I hear today's pop stars complaining of exhaustion I have to laugh. The very day Brian and I first saw the boys they were following their lunchtime gig at The Cavern with their last ever appearance in the shabby ballroom of Litherland Town Hall. They already worked incredibly hard and Brian was keen to keep up the pace. He loved the fact that they were hungry for success.

All sorts of characters emerged in the time that followed. Allan Williams has made a reputation from his association with the Beatles ever since the '50s by describing himself as the man who gave the Beatles away. However, he was never their manager. They never had a manager before Brian Epstein. Williams organised sending them to Germany for their first few tours before Brian came on the scene. Brian went to see Williams before signing them, just to see if he could learn anything. Williams told Brian not to touch them with a fucking bargepole and I remember Brian winced rather when he recounted that remark to me.

They were just exciting and fun to be with, and Brian really believed in them. Brian was a volatile, inspirational character. He took everything personally and he wanted everything to be the best. If he spotted slacking or messing around among any of his staff he just lost his temper. He didn't mean to and he knew it was wrong. But he just felt everything more strongly than anyone else I've ever known.

The Beatles were sure of one thing about their new manager – he knew how to sell records. NEMS had by then expanded to nine Liverpool record shops boasting a total stock of more than half a million records. The shops were humming with customers. Since he was so efficient at shifting records the Beatles assumed it was only a matter of time before he had a recording deal lined up for them.

Brian thought so, too. He believed in the Beatles right from the very start. It was so obvious to him that they had the talent and the potential to go right to the top.

Brian was never in the slightest doubt that Beatles records would sell in enormous quantities. He thought that if he came up with a group as good as the Beatles, then record companies would be queuing to sign them up to make records. But it was not as easy as that. Because he had conquered the retail side of the record business, he thought he was ready to take the reins as a top pop manager. But Brian's early efforts to get the Beatles a recording contract were a disaster.

Brian was meticulous about everything. Once he had dictated the detailed memos about behaviour, he had calls put in to six of his best contacts in assorted record companies. Brian was not at all put out that not one of them was instantly available and had his secretary leave messages to call him back. At that stage, he thought landing a recording contract was going to be easy. He was content to ring everyone and take the best deal offered. But the next day, Brian's elegant aura of confidence was slightly disturbed to hear that none of his contacts had returned his calls.

I recall a sharp intake of breath and Brian saying that he would have to home in on one company. 'I'll start at the top,' he smiled and rang EMI Records who then described themselves, with some justification, as 'the greatest recording organisation in the world'. As the boss of NEMS, Brian made an appointment to see Ron White who was then EMI marketing director in London. He opened the conversation by asking for additional discounts to be given for very large sales. White politely refused. Both men knew full well that EMI did not give discounts.

Then Brian revealed the real reason behind his visit. Would Ron White mind listening to a record Brian happened to have with him? This was a reversal of their usual trade but White could hardly refuse the charming Liverpool businessman. The marketing director of EMI then heard Tony Sheridan's raucous rendition of 'My Bonnie' with deafeningly enthusiastic backing from the Beat Brothers, a.k.a. the Beatles. Brian explained patiently that White should ignore Sheridan and concentrate on the support group. Brian even showed the executive a picture of the Beatles, resplendent in their original leathers, to show him what they looked like.

At the time, the Beatles were contracted to Polydor. But the contract was in German and Brian and I could not understand it. White offered to get it translated and agreed to take the record to EMI's artists and repertoire (A&R) people for their professional opinion. Brian came back to Liverpool full of optimism. But he was very naïve then. We all were. EMI listened to Brian Epstein because NEMS was a very good customer of theirs. But they were not remotely interested in Mr Epstein's questionable ability as a talent spotter. We'll get back to you.

Brian was so full of enthusiasm for the Beatles that he was not about to put all his eggs in one basket. He also contacted a couple of guys at Decca he knew well and arranged a meeting in London 'to discuss discounts' with Colin Borland, assistant to marketing chief Beecher Stevens. Brian surprised the man from Decca by quickly dismissing the subject of discounts and asking for a recording deal for the Beatles. Brian's enthusiasm was bubbling over and he backed it with the offer that if Decca recorded the Beatles then NEMS would order 5,000 copies. This was an enormous order. Plenty of singles never sold anything like that number. Brian played Borland and his boss Stevens the 'My Bonnie' record and pleaded with them to listen to the support group. Brian's belief and commitment impressed the two men from Decca enough for them to call Dick Rowe, head of A&R, who agreed, after another London meeting, to send his young assistant Mike Smith up to The Cavern to judge the Beatles for himself.

Brian was absolutely delighted. It was really something to get a London record company executive up from London. But Brian still pushed EMI as well. He wrote telling Ron White how disappointed he was not to have heard anything and warning him that Decca's man was heading north. I remember Brian noted, 'These four boys, who are superb instrumentalists, also produce some exciting and pulsating vocals. They play mostly their own compositions and one of the boys has written a song which I really believe to be the hottest material since "Living Doll".'

But White had received an emphatic thumbs down from three of EMI's four house producers and the fourth was away on holiday. So he wrote back to Brian saying, 'We feel we have sufficient groups of this type at the present time under contract and that it would not be advisable for us to sign any further contracts of this nature at present.'

Brian was devastated. He felt totally frustrated, but at least now he could pin his hopes on the visit of Mike Smith. It was 13 December 1961, and Brian took Smith to dinner before they went to The Cavern where the man from London was very impressed. Brian breathed an enormous sigh of relief when Smith raved about what he saw and heard and invited the Beatles down to London for an audition on New Year's Day 1962.

He wanted his boss Dick Rowe to see the group before he took the plunge and signed them up, but Brian was in seventh heaven. Surely now they were on their way.

There were some euphoric celebrations as we shared the good news around. I remember a session in a pub with John and he kept saying over and over again, 'We're on our way. Now we're on our way.' This had all happened so fast that it instantly cemented the relationship between the Beatles and Brian. They had been working themselves hard for years, playing endless hours in Hamburg and around Liverpool and they had never been within a sniff of a London audition. Now they were on their way.

Brian travelled down by train to London for the big day while the Beatles were driven down by their friend and 'road manager' Neil Aspinall who hired a larger van especially for the occasion. The journey took an epic ten hours as this particular band on the run got hopelessly lost in the snow somewhere near Wolverhampton. The boys were booked into 27s-a-night rooms at the Royal Hotel in Woburn Place but they were quickly traumatised by London prices. In a restaurant in the Charing Cross Road, they were astonished to discover that even the soup cost 6s and walked out. Brian prudently stayed overnight with his Aunt Frida and Uncle Berrel in Ingram Avenue, Hampstead, but he met up with his young protégés for a scotch and Coke which he had quickly learned was the Beatles' favourite drink.

The following morning, Brian was first there on the snowy opening day of 1962 and he waited with the nervous foursome for Mike Smith who was late. Punctuality was part of being professional for Brian and he struggled to hide his irritation. He felt he and the Beatles were being treated as if they did not matter. It was not a good beginning. At last their turn came, but when they produced their battered old amplifiers they were firmly told they weren't required.

Brian didn't want to ruffle too many feathers. He was keen for the Beatles to be conservative and to demonstrate their ability to deliver some standards. George sang 'The Sheikh of Araby' while Paul chipped in with a melodic version of 'Red Sails in the Sunset' and 'Like Dreamers Do'. John wanted to do more of their usual Cavern act which was full of rasping rock numbers but he allowed himself to be advised by Brian. Paul's version of "Til There Was You' went down well and Brian and the Beatles were through their nervous ordeal. The Beatles thought the session went well. Pete Best noted that Mike Smith was pleased and had said the tapes were terrific. Brian took the Beatles out to a restaurant in Swiss Cottage to celebrate.

Then followed a long period of waiting. This was very disappointing after such a promising flurry of activity since we had signed up the Beatles. We all knew they had something. But we were still unsure about what would happen next. I remember once remarking, 'There's such an awful lot of groups around nowadays,' and John snapped, 'There's such a lot of awful groups around nowadays, you mean.'

The silence from Decca was deafening. Brian was like a cat on hot bricks as he desperately tried to maintain the momentum and get an answer from Decca. His dad Harry used to get extremely irritated that Brian was always down in London chasing some record company executive or other. I would always have to try to pretend that he'd just popped to one of the other shops but I never was a very good liar.

Finally in March, after weeks of pestering for the big decision, Brian got a telephone call from Beecher Stevens inviting him to London to hear Dick Rowe's verdict. Brian was by then gloomy about the prospects. He told me, 'If it was good news, we'd have heard it by now.' In the expensive confines of Decca's seventh floor Albert Embankment executive club, the record company bosses treated Brian to a long lunch before they raised the delicate subject which was occupying his every waking thought. Then, over coffee, Dick Rowe said charmlessly, 'Not to mince words, Mr Epstein, we don't like your boys' sound. Groups are out; four-piece groups with guitarists particularly are finished.'

Brian was in a cold fury but he was determined to disguise it. He said, 'You must be out of your mind. These boys are going to explode once they appear on television. They will be bigger than the Shadows. I am completely confident that one day they will be bigger than Elvis Presley.'

Personally, I never blamed Dick Rowe, even though it was a decision that was to haunt him forever afterwards. At least he took the trouble to have the Beatles down to London to take a look at them. And he later showed that he wasn't as daft as everyone thought when he signed a scruffy-looking group called the Rolling Stones.

The Beatles were not nearly so charitable. Years later, they discovered that he had signed Brian Poole and the Tremeloes instead of them. Paul said, 'He must be kicking himself now.' And John added typically, 'I hope he kicks himself to death!'

Stevens and Rowe were startled by Brian's response that the Beatles would one day be bigger than Elvis. He wasn't the first pop figure to promise them the stars but he was the coolest and the most well-spoken. Brian found their indifference to his new charges very hard to take. Rowe went on to add, 'The boys won't go, Mr Epstein. We know these things. You have a good record business in Liverpool. Stick to that.'

Brian was determined to hide his disappointment. His faith in the Beatles kept him talking up their chances. He couldn't believe that the group that held the youth of Liverpool enraptured did not deserve to have some sort of a future in the rest of the country. He had heard the music and seen its effect. The Decca executives became a shade uneasy. Brian Epstein was a very good customer and a charming man to do business with. It would be churlish to send him back north with nothing to show for his trip. Rowe sensed it was time to soften the blow and suggested Brian should talk to Tony Meehan, the former Shadows drummer who was making a name for himself as a Decca A&R man. But the idea was that Brian would be given the benefit of Meehan's advice and the use of a studio on payment of £100.

To Brian, this was coming close to adding insult to injury. He couldn't understand why a mighty company like Decca could be asking for £100 from him for the privilege of listening to a group who could make them untold millions of pounds. But to the carefully calculating businessman in Brian, it was impossible to turn down the only concession he had won from Decca.

So the next day, Brian arrived at Decca's West Hampstead studios and, after again being kept waiting for half-an-hour, Dick Rowe said, 'Tony, take Mr Epstein out and explain the position.' Brian was starting to feel as if he was back at one of his prep schools, in deep trouble with his housemaster again.

Tony Meehan had encountered plenty of managers with astronomic aspirations for their groups and tersely told Brian, 'Mr Epstein, Mr Rowe and I are very busy men. We know roughly what you require so will you fix a date for tapes to be made of these Beatles. Telephone my secretary to make sure that when you want the session I am available.'

Brian was seething inwardly. He walked out of Decca full of frustration and fury. It was so blindingly obvious to him by then that the Beatles were stars of the future. He simply could not believe that anyone, let alone senior executives of a successful record company, could not grasp this simple fact. He decided not to take Meehan up on his half-hearted offer of help. And he was crestfallen that he had to break the bad news to the boys.

Brian tried to hide his feelings when he came back but I knew him pretty well by then and I could see he was deeply upset. He attempted to put on a brave front for the boys. When his train got back into Liverpool's Lime Street Station he telephoned Paul and asked him to round the boys up for a meeting in Joe's Café in Duke Street. There, over a tidal flow of tea, they talked for a time about everything but the crucial Decca verdict, until George asked, 'What about Decca, Brian?'

'I'm afraid it's no use,' said Brian. 'I've had a flat "No".'

They took it pretty well, but then they had been trying to break through for a long time before we arrived. Brian found rejection much harder to take. He began a round of trips to London and meetings with executives from Pye, Phillips and other smaller companies and they all turned him down flat. I often used to find him crying in his office. He could not understand why none of them could hear what he could hear in the tapes. But they were tears of anger and frustration, not sorrow. He just could not understand why no one could see what was so obvious to him.

The boys seemed able to hide their feelings with humour. With the nonchalance of youth, at times they would send up the whole idea of getting to the top. John had a jokey routine where he would shout, 'Where are we going, fellas?'

The others would shout back, 'To the top, Johnny.'

'What top?' he'd shout.

And they would yell, 'To the Toppermost of the Poppermost, Johnny!'

On the local scene, the Beatles were going from strength to strength. They were busy most nights playing for Brian's new minimum rate of £15 per night. And they came top of a Mersey Beat popularity poll, thanks largely to them filling in loads of entry forms under assumed names putting the Beatles first and their main rivals Gerry and the Pacemakers last. Mind you, all the groups were voting for themselves so it hardly altered the vote, but Brian was quick to use the triumph for publicity purposes. For an appearance on 24 March 1962, posters screamed in huge capital letters that they were 'MERSEY BEAT POLL WINNERS! POLYDOR RECORDING ARTISTS! PRIOR TO EUROPEAN TOUR!' The fact that the concert was at Barnston Women's Institute with tickets priced at 7s 6d was surprisingly given rather less prominence.

The European Tour was, in fact, their third visit to Hamburg in April 1962. Before Brian and I met them, the boys had undertaken two wild stints of working in Hamburg. They had travelled over in an old van and worked excruciating hours, lived in squalid circumstances and generally experimented with as many aspects of the local low-life as they had time for.

This time, they flew to Hamburg which was a first for the boys, and they loved it. They were playing the Star Club, which was definitely a step up from the previous venues they used to play. 'It even had proper curtains on stage,' said George.

But back in Liverpool, Brian was really up against it. His father was by now seriously irritated that Brian was spending his time obsessed by this group of scruffy musicians when he should have been running the shops. Harry was very polite. He would come into the shop, find me in charge, and launch into a string of direct questions: 'Alistair, are the record stocks sufficient?' 'Alistair, did you order enough copies of that record?' 'Alistair, are the staff being managed adequately?' 'Alistair, could you tell me just exactly where Brian is, please?'

But there was no diverting Brian. He was dedicated to getting the boys launched. I had come to respect his musical judgement so much by then that I shared his frustration and impatience.

The first Beatles engagement under the new Epstein contract was at the Thistle Café on the seafront at upmarket West Kirby some ten miles from Liverpool. The Beatles fee was £18 and Brian took his 36s commission which he noted, 'just about covered petrol, oil and wear on tyres'. It wasn't exactly the big-time.

At the Aintree Institute, Brian received the £15 fee in bags of silver coins which horrified him. He angrily told promoter Brian Kelly that the Beatles must be paid in a civilised manner. He stalked off leaving the coins behind and shouted, 'Send me a cheque,' over his shoulder as he went out of the room in undisguised disgust.

People like Bill Harry – who was a friend of John's at art college – have suggested that this was the time when Brian changed the Beatles from being John's group into being Paul's group. Bill reckons John's position as the early leader was gradually usurped by Paul, with Brian's help. To me, this has never sounded convincing. One of the important qualities of the Beatles when I first met them was that they did not have a leader. Perhaps the drummer was always taking a back seat by necessity. Pete Best – and later, Ringo Starr – were both quiet, easy-going guys by nature. And they had to be at the back because that's where the drums were and John, George and Paul were always out front. John had been the leader in the early days certainly, but by the time Brian became involved in 1961 it seemed like a genuine partnership to me.

Indeed, the thing that made the Beatles so great in those early days was their strong sense of togetherness. After years of struggling through grotty clubs and battling along through those endless Hamburg sessions, John, Paul and George were rock solid.

Brian loved the way the Beatles were so completely unconventional. They weren't remotely like Cliff Richard and the Shadows, heaven forbid, or even Gerry and the

Pacemakers. They were four different, highly-talented people who would probably have done perfectly well as individuals. But as a team they were absolutely unbeatable. It never was John's group and it never became Paul's group. The last thing Brian wanted the Beatles to do was have any leader other than himself.

We went together to watch an early concert over the river at the Tower Ballroom, New Brighton. It was a huge hall which could hold more than 1,000 people. The Beatles were sharing the bill with three other local groups – Rory Storm and the Hurricanes, Derry and the Seniors, and Dale Roberts and the Jaywalkers. There was just no competition. The Beatles were phenomenal. Now they had taken on board Brian's tips about smartening up their appearance and their act they simply oozed confidence on stage. Brian and I shared a table at the side while the boys performed and the improvement in the look and the sound of the boys was so extraordinary that we simply could not keep from grinning at each other. We were delighted with what we saw and heard.

Brain faced pressure from all sides and it didn't always make him easy to work for. I was sacked several times in the '60s. The first occasion was the most frightening, because I thought he really meant it.

The day had started like many others. Brian came rushing in first thing, announcing he was going to be out all day. I was in charge. About five minutes later, the phone in his office rang and I rushed through to answer it. It was good news, a booking for the Beatles! I glanced through Brian's big desk diary and saw that there was nothing already booked. 'That's fine,' I said. 'Just send us the contracts for the booking and we'll have them to you by return.'

My trouble started when I couldn't find a pen. I'd left it in the shop. All I had was a pencil, so I took a note on a piece of scrap paper intending to transfer it later neatly into the diary in pen, as Brian preferred. You've guessed it. I forgot.

It was a very busy day and towards closing time I took another call for the Beatles and duly wrote it into the diary which seemed clear for that day. Brian returned and generously said, 'You look shattered. Go on home and put your feet up.'

I didn't need to be told twice. But the next morning, when I arrived Brian came over to me and hissed, 'Alistair, I want to see you in my office at once.' He had that tight, carefully-controlled look which comes over him when he is angry. So I left everything and followed him to the back office, wondering what was wrong. There were two contracts laid out on Brian's desk. He stood behind the desk and pointed to them as if they were my death warrants.

'Alistair, these are two contracts which came to me this morning from different promoters. They are both for the same night at clubs which are 15 miles apart! The Beatles cannot possibly fulfil both bookings! What explanation can you give me which might prevent me asking for your resignation?'

I was baffled. I looked at the contracts. Surely I had never done anything so stupid. Then I remembered I had written down the details of the first booking on the piece of paper and forgotten to transfer them to the desk diary. The second booking was the one I had written in. I fished in my pocket and found the crumpled piece of paper.

'Well, Brian ...'

Brian was furious. His voice was shaking with rage as he delivered the most stinging lecture I'd heard since I left school. He said, 'Do you realise that our professional reputation as managers depends on us keeping our word and fulfilling our bookings? How can we expect anyone to take us seriously if we act like clowns? Everything has to be done properly and I will accept no excuses. What you did has cast a shadow on the reputation not only of me but also of the Beatles. It is up to you to remedy the situation at once. Your job depends upon it.'

Fortunately for me, the first promoter I rang happily accepted my snivelling apology and agreed to reschedule the Beatles for another night. He said, 'Don't worry, we get double bookings all the time. We'll get another group for that night. The kids will never notice.'

I could have kissed him down the line, even if I did not think much of his musical taste. I was still trembling as I put the phone down. But Brian had made his point.

I was still feeling wretched and offered to resign if he thought I was not up to doing my job. Brian had now reverted to the charming chap I thought I knew so well. 'Alistair, I don't want your resignation. You are essential to the running of this whole project and I am sorry if I have been overloading you. I hope it won't be for too long because I intend to break out of Liverpool and move to London as soon as possible. With your help, I want to put the Beatles at the very top of the music business. But remember, no more mistakes.'

I got the message. Brian was an inspirational boss and he never asked anyone to work harder than he was prepared to slave himself. He desperately strived to stay 100 per cent on top of things at the shop and still found time to go off to London to find someone in the record business who shared his high opinion of the Beatles. But the knock-backs continued.

At Pye, he was rejected by genial artists' manager Alan A Freeman who said Brian's tape from the Decca audition was not good enough, although he might consider listening again to a better presentation. Brian tried the independent label Oriole, but boss Morris Levy was out and Brian's time in London was very limited. He telephoned Philips Records to ask if he could meet an executive and a secretary told him coldly to 'write in'.

Brian spent hours on the train to London and back and he found it desperately disheartening not to return with better news. As the weeks went by, Brian became increasingly depressed and gradually the attitude of the Beatles began to change. There was a shade more edge in their questions when he returned and John and Paul particularly started to lose faith.

They didn't blame Brian to his face, but among themselves and sometimes to me they would question what was happening. John asked me if I thought they'd ever get a deal and I tried to be upbeat and explain that Brian was doing everything possible but they seemed less and less convinced.

Every month, Brian would issue each of the boys with their financial statements, all neatly and accurately itemised, and sealed in a white manila envelope. They reacted very differently. John would instantly crumple it up and stuff it in his pocket. George might have a look. Ringo certainly couldn't understand it and didn't waste any time trying. Paul was the one who opened it carefully and would sit in the corner of the office for hours going meticulously though it. He would read every detail and question Brian on anything he didn't understand.

It was May 1962 when the breakthrough came, just six months after Brian and I had walked into The Cavern and seen this explosion of raw talent. The Beatles were in Hamburg and Brian was making another visit to London. I sensed that he was getting near the end of the road. He was always very down when he had had to disappoint the boys with the news from London yet again. We would sit in his office late into the night sometimes and tears would come into his eyes as he would go through yet another unproductive encounter.

'The main qualification to run a record company seems to be cotton wool in your ears,' said Brian. He named one particular record company minor executive and said he was 'a complete bastard. He actually suggested that if I put my money where my mouth is then a deal might be possible. I said I had already spent hundreds of pounds trying to get the Beatles a record deal. He just smiled and said what he really meant was that I should put my money where his bank account was. I couldn't believe it. I never thought I was a particularly honest or upright man, but to hear this slithery, time-serving creep actually ask for a bribe made my flesh crawl. If I was the violent type, I think I might even have struck him.'

By the time the vital contact was made, Brian was pretty desperate. He knew that he was running out of time with the Beatles. He never lost faith in them but he knew that if he didn't break them on to the national scene then someone would come along who would do just that.

On 8 May, he made what he told me was possibly his last London sales trip. 'I don't think I can keep doing this for ever, Alistair,' he told me with a faltering voice the night before he went. 'I think some of the record companies laugh at me and I'm afraid the boys are beginning to see the joke. I feel like the only man in the regiment who is in step! Could it be that I'm the one who is out of line here?'

He was so desperate by then that he was talking to anyone in London with the remotest connection to getting a record deal. He went to visit Robert Boast, who was general manager of the Oxford Street HMV shop. He'd met Robert Boast on a sales training course in Germany organised by Deutsche Grammophon a year earlier. He knew Boast couldn't hand out recording contracts but he was there to ask if there was anyone at EMI he could put him in touch with. Brian asked Boast to transfer his well-used tape on to an acetate record which they could do in the shop. Boast said frankly that the Beatles were not to his taste but, not knowing of Brian's endless round of rejections, he suggested someone at EMI who should listen to it.

Boast's recording engineer, Jim Foy, enjoyed the music and telephoned Sid Coleman, who ran EMI's publishing arm from his office up on the fourth floor.

When Brian duly played the tapes in his office, Coleman was instantly impressed. 'Have you taken these to anyone?' he asked.

'Yes,' Brian said with feeling. 'Everybody! But I'm still trying.'

'Have you taken them to George Martin?'

'Who's George Martin?' asked Brian, who was beginning to feel as if he was trapped in a revolving door. But George

Martin turned out to be the fourth EMI house producer who had been on holiday when the other three all turned down the Beatles. The helpful Sid Coleman rang George Martin and a meeting was fixed up with Brian for the following day.

Brian realised that he was reaching the end of the road with record companies. There are only so many doors even the most enthusiastic salesman is prepared to have slammed in his face. He rang me to explain what had happened, that he would be staying down another night, and I detected a weariness in his voice. He was fed up with failure and tired of rejection. Brian was very down and I tried to say that this George Martin might be just the man they needed. I think, in a way, he was in two minds about staying down in London. Doubt had set in and he was beginning to wonder if he really was such an infallible judge of public pop taste as he'd come to believe.

'Maybe we should just sell records, Alistair?' he said, weighing up the options open to him. 'We don't seem to be very successful at making them.'

It had to be worth one more try and that was what I told Brian with as much positive energy in my voice as I could muster.

Brian spent that night before he met George Martin with his aunt and uncle in Hampstead. There he appeared down-hearted and close to accepting defeat in his long battle to become a showbusiness impresario. He admitted to his kind-hearted Uncle Berrel that he was becoming despondent after all the rejections. His conviction that the Beatles were a wonderful act remained, but he was wondering whether he was really the man to manage them. He was getting nowhere fast and was considering giving up even before his meeting with George Martin. 'What shall I do?' he asked Uncle Berrel. 'I've got one more appointment but I don't know what to do. Shall I give it all up and go home?'

Berrel was baffled by his smart young nephew's indecision, but wisely counselled, 'Oh, just keep that last appointment.'

When Brian arrived at EMI's Abbey Road studios, his mood had lifted and he spoke eloquently and passionately about the four young men called the Beatles and their amazing talents as writers and performers. George Martin was a tall, well-spoken man who was every bit as smart and sophisticated as Brian. Martin was hardly typical of the racy pop record scene. His success had come largely in comedy records at EMI as the recording manager of the zany *Goon Show* stars Peter Sellers and Spike Milligan and of top ballad singer Matt Monro. The two men quickly established a mutual respect and George Martin decided to take a chance on the very rare material. 'OK,' said Martin. 'Bring them down to London and I'll give them a test.'

At least that was Brian's story. But it is not quite the whole story. What was not known at the time was that Brian Epstein blackmailed EMI into taking the Beatles. George Martin finished up with the Beatles because Brian Epstein threatened to stop dealing with EMI. Brian was so close to the end of his tether that he put as much commercial pressure as he could muster on EMI to make them give the Beatles a chance. Put plain and simply, that is blackmail. Brian threatened to withdraw his business from EMI if they didn't give the Beatles a recording contract. It was as simple as that. He went to every record company but, in the end, to George Martin on Parlophone which was not a major pop label. It turned out to be a heaven-sent partnership between George Martin and the Beatles.

But George Martin was a classical musician who, although realising the group's talent, most certainly was not dying to record with four scruffs from Liverpool. Pressure from high up in EMI probably also helped to make sure they did not lose Mr Epstein's business. Brian and I had already talked about how NEMS would ditch EMI's HMV, Parlophone and Columbia labels. There was not much on the HMV label that worried us and we could get Parlophone and Columbia when needed. As it turned out, it was a stroke of genius putting George Martin with the Beatles but it was caused by Brian saying, 'Give me a contract.'

But the deal, when it came, was lousy. They paid a penny a record for the greatest group the world has ever seen. Brian re-negotiated it later. But we all just wanted that crucial first recording contract. That was what mattered. Not the royalties. Not the percentage. Just please, please give us a contract.

Brian hurried away from the Abbey Road studios and sent two telegrams. One went to the Beatles in Hamburg and said, 'Congratulations, boys. EMI request recording session. Please rehearse new material.' The second went to *Mersey Beat* newspaper in Liverpool: 'Have secured contract for Beatles to record for EMI on Parlophone label. First recording date set for 6 June.' The news quickly went round Liverpool. The Beatles were on their way.

It wasn't really a recording contract, it was an audition. But the Beatles soon realised that. They played 'Love Me

Do', 'PS I Love You', 'Ask Me Why', 'Besame Mucho', and the old Fats Waller song 'Your Feet's Too Big'. George Martin liked what he heard and was just as impressed by the humour and personality of the boys. Afterwards, they adjourned to the Alpino restaurant in Marylebone High Street. 'OK, I like you. We'll make some records.'

But even then it wasn't easy. George Martin is a nice fella but I saw Brian reduced to tears of anger and frustration afterwards when promised telephone calls confirming they really were on the next step of the ladder did not come through. Brian was just about the coolest customer I've ever known, but some nights he used to be in the shop late at night waiting and waiting and waiting for that vital phone call and he would end up thumping the desk in despair.

'He's promised to ring,' he would say. 'Why doesn't he ring? What has gone wrong now?'

It meant so much to Brian to get this group launched. It wasn't the money he was going to have. It wasn't the fame he wanted to enjoy. He just knew they had that special ingredient that deserved to make them into superstars before the word had even been invented. He used to get very, very emotional. Tears would run down his face and he'd say, 'Why will they not ring me?' Of course, the Beatles never, ever saw Brian Epstein like that.

I always knew when he was really down because he'd say, 'Alistair, can we have dinner?' I'd ring Lesley and warn her that she wasn't going to see me until late. We used to go out and he would pour his heart out. He wasn't in love with John. That wasn't it at all. The whole sexual side of Brian's nature has been exaggerated and invented so comprehensively and so ludicrously. It wasn't sexual. It was that he had found something special. And he had moulded it. He had put them into suits and he had taught them how to behave and to smile. And he knew they could be bigger than Elvis. It was his dream to make them take over the world. Sure, he loved John. But he also loved Paul and George. We knew what the future would be. We used to talk with the Beatles of world tours and ticker-tape welcomes and endless parties. Brian knew it would all come true. That's why he became so furious when anyone got in the way.

Eventually, at the end of July, confirmation of George Martin's plans for a recording session came through. Brian told John and Paul and they told George. But no one told Pete Best. The Beatles had decided their drummer was not up to scratch.

Brian said that George Martin had criticised Pete's drumming and that the other three Beatles had come to feel his beat was not right for their music. He tried to persuade them to leave the group as it was, but they somehow thought Pete was too conventional to be a Beatle. He was friendly with John but not with Paul and George and the three of them made a joint approach to Brian so he was forced to act.

It had to be done quickly and decisively and I know Brian had a sleepless night before the confrontation. Brian hated giving bad news to anyone, but he had no choice. Having met up with Pete at the office on 16 August, he told him, 'I've got some bad news for you. The boys want you out and Ringo in.'

Pete was dumbstruck, and to this day I think he is still pretty puzzled about how they could do that to someone who had been on the road with them for two years.

He tried to soften the blow by telling Pete that he would be the star of a new group he would be forming, but Pete knew as well as Brian that the Beatles were going to be something special. For the faithful Neil Aspinall, this was a very difficult time. He was a great friend of the Best family, but he did not let that stand in the way of sticking with the Beatles.

Brian always let this be seen as a musical decision taken by the Beatles themselves. And, in a way, it was, yet Brian and I had several times talked in our distinctly unmusical way about something being not quite right about Pete's drumming. We tried to put our finger on Pete's weaknesses but we failed to identify them.

Brian was not surprised when the boys came to him to do their dirty work. Deep down he agreed with the decision; indeed, he and I were both flattered to have come to the same conclusion as the Beatles. Brian certainly would not have sacked Pete otherwise, but he said to me that he knew the boys were absolutely right. And he was certain that Ringo was a definite improvement, not least because he was a great deal more malleable than Pete. Brian had crossed swords with Pete about not combing his hair like the other guys. But then Pete always was something of the odd man out. From the very first time we saw them, John, Paul and George had a jokey rapport both on stage and off that Pete clearly did not share. He was a terribly nice fella but he would be sulking when the other three were laughing. Technically, Pete was a better drummer than Ringo but he was not right for the Beatles.

Evidently, George Martin felt Pete's drumming was not quite up to scratch and the other three felt that he did not quite fit in. To add insult to injury, Brian asked him to stay on until the end of the week, for two more nights, until

Ringo arrived. Brian had already contacted Ringo, who was playing drums for Rory Storm and the Hurricanes on summer season at Butlin's in Skegness. Brian, and then later John Lennon, rang the holiday camp and had a message broadcast over the public address system for Richard Starkey to come to the phone. Luckily for Brian, Ringo was already unsettled with the Hurricanes and agreed to the move for an initial salary of £25 per week. Ringo was delighted. He had already sat in with the Beatles at a couple of Cavern sessions when Pete Best had been ill. He gave a disgruntled Rory Storm just three days' notice and on Saturday, 18 August 1962, he took his place behind the drum kit at the Hulme Hall in Port Sunlight near Birkenhead.

The fans were not happy. For a time, Beatles followers were in revolt all over Liverpool. Brian kept away from The Cavern where enthusiasts who preferred the original line-up chanted, 'Pete for Ever, Ringo Never', waved banners and caused some unpleasant scenes. Brian took to using the services of a burly bodyguard for a time and George Harrison, who didn't, was given a black eye by one disenchanted fan.

But Ringo settled in well. It was John who explained to him that he would have to get rid of his trademark beard, though he could keep his 'sidies'. It seems a traumatic event even now, but this was in a summer packed full of change.

In June, Brian had signed up possibly the second-best group in Liverpool as well as the best when he agreed to manage Gerry and the Pacemakers. Gerry was quickly followed by Billy J Kramer and the Dakotas and The Big Three. Brian and his brother Clive became directors of the new company, NEMS Enterprises Ltd, which was formed to incorporate all of his showbiz expansion.

The Beatles appeared on television for the first time when Granada TV cameras filmed them in action at The Cavern. John Lennon married his very charming and very pregnant girlfriend Cynthia Powell and Brian hosted a discreet 'wedding lunch' at Reece's cafeteria. But neither Brian nor John wanted the marriage to get in the way of the business and John started his wedding night on stage with the Beatles at Chester's Riverpark Ballroom.

Most significant of all, under the experienced care of George Martin, the Beatles recorded their historic first record, 'Love Me Do', in two sessions on 4 and 11 September. Ringo was upset that George Martin had installed experienced session drummer Andy White for the recording.

Martin still did not know quite what to make of the Beatles but he was anxious to put them at their ease. Before they started work, he asked, 'Let me know if there is anything you don't like.' He wasn't really expecting a reply, but George Harrison said, 'Well, for a start, I don't like your tie.' This joke baffled more than amused Martin, who felt he was looking smart for work as usual. But everyone laughed and the session got under way.

It took more than 15 takes to record 'Love Me Do' to George Martin's satisfaction. Then they started work on the flipside which was 'PS I Love You'. Ringo was relegated to tambourine and maracas and was beginning to wonder if he was about to suffer the same fate as poor Pete Best. Afterwards, he was very down and told me, 'What a fucking liberty. How can they say it's by the Beatles if they get other musicians in. What a phoney business.'

Brian listened to the acetates the next day in George Martin's office at EMI headquarters in Manchester Square. Brian was in seventh heaven. He felt it had gone absolutely brilliantly and raved about the harmonica work.

THE BIG BREAK
5

'Love Me Do' was released on 4 October 1962 and the sales took off instantly – but only in Liverpool. Beatles fans deluged radio request programmes with demands to hear the song and the national reaction was rather slower. But a week after release, it stood at number 49 in the *Record* retailer chart. The boys were absolutely ecstatic. I think they were happier about that than I ever saw them.

John just stood and looked at the chart and looked at me and said, 'They're buying our record. Real people are buying our fucking record.' For all the knockout live concerts they had given, they knew that those only led to another concert. They knew selling records was their passport to stardom. I remember John singing away to himself about being a '49er'. Sales improved slowly and erratically until the end of the year, when the Beatles' first record peaked at number 17 on 27 December. It was a really encouraging start.

Brian was buoyed up by this relative success. But there was a strong suspicion in Liverpool and in the business that Brian had hyped the record into the charts. People said that he had bought piles of copies, some 10,000 the rumours said.

Brian denied it emphatically and he was telling the truth. Brian Epstein was the most honest man I ever knew but, perhaps because he was so successful, people who never knew him imagined him ducking and diving like some sort of seedy spiv. He wasn't like that. There were requests for backhanders over the years certainly, but Brian simply refused or, better still, ignored them.

Years later, when he and the Beatles had more money than any of them would ever spend, I was managing, on his behalf, a fabulous folk group called The Silkie. We had a load of lucrative bookings in America but because they were not well known over there we could not get work permits for them. I was introduced to this mysterious lawyer. He looked like something out of a gangster film and he was a very powerful man. He told me that, for $1,000 in cash, he could get work permits with no questions asked. I thought this was the answer and asked Brian for the money.

'Alistair,' he said, 'I have never paid over bribes or illicit money to anyone and I am not about to start now.'

'Love Me Do' changed everything. The first record might have peaked at a modest 17, but it launched the group on to a new level and it registered their astonishing ability to shrewd observers. The Beatles were suddenly wanted on television on Granada's *People and Places* which was a regional programme for the north that went out from Manchester. The Beatles went down well and then had to dash off to Hamburg for two previously booked fortnights of live appearances. The whirlwind of excitement was really starting to blow at the time. Brian was on a permanent high. The boys kept coming into the shop, as if there were going to be daily bulletins on their rise to super stardom.

George Martin was pleased with the success but totally won over to Brian's view that the boys had it in them to be something very special. The most important task was to find a follow-up record which would build on the sales of 'Love Me Do'.

Mitch Murray sent in a catchy little song to George Martin called 'How Do You Do It?' George thought it was definite hit material. The Beatles tried it out and hated it. Gerry Marsden couldn't agree less and turned it into a number-one hit. The boys didn't regret their decision. 'Lots of shit rises to the top of the charts,' observed John laconically one night. 'We don't do shit.'

There was a lot of rivalry between the groups in those days. Gerry felt with some justification that Brian concentrated all his efforts on the Beatles and the boys frankly thought they were a whole lot better than Gerry and the Pacemakers. When the Beatles rejected 'How Do You Do It?' George Martin was annoyed and told them that if the song wasn't good enough for them then they had better come up with something that was acceptable. And quickly.

'Please, Please Me' was the Beatles response to the challenge. It was the song that changed everything. It was released on 11 January 1963 and by 22 February it was number one. Admittedly, it initially shared the prized top spot with Frank Ifield's 'The Wayward Wind'. 1963 was the year the rest of the country discovered what the people of Liverpool had known for some time, that the Beatles were simply the greatest group the world has ever seen.

This was the time that Brian had been waiting and hoping and planning for. The Beatles worked incredibly hard as Brian put them through 12 months of the toughest and most punishing schedule of concert tours, one-night appearances, recording sessions, radio recordings, television appearances, photograph sessions and Press interviews. The Beatles did everything that was asked of them and Brian asked an awful lot.

They obeyed Brian's rules about behaviour to the letter. Well, almost. The boys always liked a drink as they performed and alcohol was banned at Granada cinemas where many of the concerts were held. They got round this by taking in Coca Cola which had already been heavily laced with whisky. I'd never heard of scotch and Coke before I met the boys, so to me it always seemed like a Beatles' invention.

But with a record at the top of the charts they knew this was the moment they had been waiting for since the three of them got together as schoolboys. And Ringo knew enough to do as he was told. The boys' emergence on to the national stage did not please all of their most fervent Liverpool fans who realised early on that they would see less of their favourites in future as they moved out of the grasp of Merseyside. Local legend has it that when the news of their first number one was announced at The Cavern, it was greeted with stony silence. But there wasn't much silence in the office as interest in the boys spiralled amazingly.

Gerry and the Pacemakers, Billy J Kramer and the Dakotas, and The Big Three started having hits as well and the whole world just went completely mad for a while. Phones rang constantly. More secretaries and assistants arrived and went as Brian struggled to stay in control. The boys were on tour with Helen Shapiro. When it began, she was the star of the show, but by the time it had finished the screams for the Beatles drowned out just about everything else.

In April, they released 'From Me To You' which was written by John and Paul on the coach during their Helen Shapiro tour. The first LP, *Please, Please Me*, included both sides of their first two records, as well as 'Twist and Shout' and 'A Taste of Honey'. Both single and LP shot to the top of the charts and the Beatles were booked for another exhausting tour in May, this time with Roy Orbison. At the start, Orbison topped the bill and the Beatles were all impressed by his amazing voice. But as the Beatles' popularity grew and grew, the positions were reversed, and they followed The Big O. This was right because of their fanatical following, but Roy Orbison was such a great singer that his final version of 'Pretty Woman' had the fans on their feet. The Beatles were left behind the curtain wondering how on earth they were going to follow that. But they did it every time.

They could do anything and John could do more than the others. He might have left a lasting image as an anarchic rebel but I can remember clearly how excited he was when the Beatles were asked to appear on the *Morecambe and Wise* show.

I did have a scare at the *NME* Awards night when the Shadows were announced, at which the Beatles all leaped up and cheered and I was scared they were going to start taking the mickey. But they were serious. They would not have crossed the road to listen to Cliff Richard but they wanted to see the Shadows in action because they had always admired their musicianship. 'You see, Al, we're not taking the piss all the time,' said John. They just stood at the side of the stage watching in appreciation.

The boys enjoyed their fame. In those days, Brian was always keen that they should know whenever a Beatles record was going to be played on the radio. I'd pass on the information and they would stop the car, or whatever they were doing, to listen. The Beatles would have special celebration dinners for every number one. Brian loved to reward them for doing well. And as the money poured in, they started to eat a lot better as well. In that first couple of years of success, they all steadily put on a little weight. They say a true Beatles fanatic can tell from a photograph just when in that period it was taken!

These were the most amazing times for the Beatles because the public discovered them before the newspapers. There were massive crowds everywhere they performed and riots to get near them became a constant problem for the boys. George unwisely mentioned that he liked jelly babies and the fans hurled millions of the sweets at them whenever they could.

There was a real closeness between the boys in those heady early days. They felt like they were taking on the whole world and all they needed was each other. They had their own private language and a sense of humour that was all their own. If anyone was being boring in the dressing room, the Beatles had a code for getting rid of them. They would just catch roadie Mal Evans' eye and yawn in the appropriate direction and the bore would be swiftly steered towards the exit.

But the national Press remained largely uninterested for a long time. Maureen Cleave of the London *Evening Standard* had done one of the earliest London interviews in February when she marvelled at their humour and freshness and described their famous fringes as a French hairstyle. Brian was desperate to get more national paper coverage but it didn't really arrive in a big way until the autumn. It was completely the other way round from today when tedious, talentless unknowns are hyped into the charts by carefully orchestrated Press, TV and radio campaigns. The Beatles had to earn their amazing national following the hard way.

But when it came to performing or recording, they were fantastic. They recorded their first album, *Please, Please*

Me, in one remarkable 12-hour session at Abbey Road. George Martin was trying to capture live the sort of excitement the Beatles generated in their live performances in Liverpool or Hamburg. That album is still one of my favourites and I'm always amazed that John's throat holds out for the final raucous rendition of 'Twist and Shout'. John said that last effort almost killed him and his throat took months to recover. He drank pints and pints of milk because he thought it would help. In the end, they were happy with the result and it still sounds great to me today. Paul loved working at Abbey Road so much it was one of the reasons he bought a house round the corner in Cavendish Avenue.

One story the Press certainly didn't get at the time was that in April, in the middle of the euphoria that followed all the early success and acclaim, Brian and John went off to Spain for a holiday. So much invention and rubbish has been made of this trip by so many people since, that the truth deserves at least a brief mention. The most sensational version, of course, is that the holiday was a chance for Brian to consummate his overwhelming passion for John, which inspired him to sign the group in the first place. I'm afraid it wasn't like that.

John roared with laughter at the rumours that began afterwards. Typically, he encouraged the stories that he and Brian were gay lovers because he thought it was funny and John was one of the world's great wind-up merchants. He told me afterwards in one of our frankest heart-to-hearts that Brian never seriously did proposition him. He had teased Brian about the young men he kept gazing at and the odd ones who had found their way to his room. Brian had joked to John about the women who hurled themselves at him. 'If he'd asked me, I probably would have done anything he wanted. I was so much in awe of Brian then I'd have tried a night of vice-versa. But he never wanted me like that. Sure, I took the mickey a bit and pretended to lead him on. But we both knew we were joking. He wanted a pal he could have a laugh with and someone he could teach about life. I thought his bum boys were creeps and Brian knew that. Even completely out of my head, I couldn't shag a bloke. And I certainly couldn't lie there and let one shag me. Even a nice guy like Brian. To be honest, the thought of it turns me over.'

All the same, John was very selfish to have gone off on holiday with Brian then because it was just after Cynthia had given birth to his son Julian. John's whole romance and marriage to Cynthia was kept a secret at the time because Brian feared the effect of publicity about one of the Beatles having a wife, let alone a family.

The Beatles were on tour in April 1963 when Cynthia went into labour in Liverpool's Sefton General Hospital and it was a week before John even went to see Julian. John used to ring Mimi every night for reports on the baby and Brian had arranged a private room for Cynthia for a remarkable 25s a day. John tried to disguise himself to avoid publicity when he eventually went to see his wife and son and Cynthia laughed at him when she saw the fake moustache, hat and dark glasses. But it was still a wonderful moment for her as John rushed into her room and told her how clever she was. His first question was, 'Who does he look like?'

Julian had suffered from jaundice when he was born but the yellow colour had subsided by then. John took Julian in his arms and said, 'He's bloody marvellous, Cyn, isn't he absolutely fantastic?'

But even this intimate family moment was interrupted because the private room had a window on to the main ward and one of the mothers shouted, 'It's him. One of the Beatles.' John's cover was blown and he told Cyn he would have to go to avoid a fuss. He just had time to tell her that he wanted Brian to be the baby's godfather and he and Brian were taking a holiday in Spain at the end of an exhausting tour.

Cynthia told me afterwards that she was very shocked by this whole experience. Her most personal moment with her husband and their new baby had been hijacked by fans screaming at them through the window, and John had reacted by running off on holiday with his manager. Cyn knew perfectly well that John didn't have a homosexual inclination in his body, but she still didn't like being left quite literally holding the baby. But when she questioned her husband's holiday plans, John snorted, 'Being selfish again, aren't you? I've been working my ass off for months on one-night stands. Those people staring from the other side of the glass are bloody everywhere, haunting me. I deserve a holiday. And, anyway, Brian wants me to go, and I owe it to the poor guy. Who else does he have to go away with?'

Since then, one or two so-called 'friends' have come out of the woodwork to say that John told them he slept with Brian on the trip to Barcelona. I don't believe it. When Paul was asked years later about the incident, after all the aggro and acrimony had long since spoiled the relationship, he said John had never said anything to him about sleeping with Brian. If it had happened, he would have known. I'm sure if there was anything to tell, it would have been Paul John would have told. Forget what happened later – at that time, they were closer than any two men I've ever known. The four Beatles were all rock solid mates in those early days. That's how they got through it all. But John and Paul were like brothers. In fact, they were a lot closer than most brothers.

I asked John about it because I couldn't ask Brian and because I wanted to know what happened. I also knew that Brian did have a weakness for what is charmlessly known as a 'bit of rough'. All the problems he encountered in his life followed from taking into his home or his hotel room guys with a certain basic earthy charm. I suppose John could have come into that category. He could certainly be rough, but I believe Brian's relationship with the Beatles was stronger and more important to him than any sexual thing. He did love the Beatles, all of them, but not in that way, I'm absolutely convinced of it.

THE PRICE OF FAME
6

At the time of Brian's holiday with John, we had just had our first taste of success. That was what Brian had been striving for. He was starting to see his dream come true. He knew the Beatles could take over the world. He knew they could become bigger than Elvis, and this was the ambition that sustained him. Once we had seen them at The Cavern, Brian was absolutely sure the Beatles could make it. That was his mission and he wasn't going to ruin it by risking antagonising John. Brian used to say to me that John was the genius of the Beatles and he was incredibly excited about John's talent. Brian used to say, 'Sometimes when they play, the hairs on the back of my neck stand up on end. They're electrifying.' It was beyond money. He wanted the world to see what he could see – the talent of the Beatles.

In any case, if Brian had been planning to try it on with John he would never ever have openly taken him on holiday. He took me on holiday several times to show his appreciation of my work. It was his way of saying thank you. But we always had separate rooms and the thought that he might knock on my door in the middle of the night never crossed my mind. I worked closely with Brian from the start of the '60s until his death and he never once gave me any actual concrete evidence that he was gay. Times were different then. Homosexuality was illegal and undercover and not spoken about. Brian honestly thought that people did not know he was gay. He was much too discreet for that. Brian was so aware of the importance of the Beatles' public image, and he was also worried about the impact of the knowledge that John had a wife would have on the group's popularity. The idea that John Lennon was a 'queer' would have been totally abhorrent to Brian.

Before he left for the holiday, Brian got me to make sure Cynthia received a brand-new Silver Cross pram. He was very moved that John had asked him to be Julian's godfather and he certainly intended to take his responsibilities seriously. He felt very sorry that Cynthia had been sidelined so effectively. She was a very nice person and Brian often said how good an influence she was on John. But it suited the grand plan to keep her well in the background, baby and all. They lived as quietly as possible with John's Aunt Mimi in Liverpool.

Brian took John to Spain because he wanted to share with him his great love – bullfighting. The colour and the violence and the spectacle of the gruesome sport was something that Brian really loved. He knew it would impress John and it did. Brian told me that John hadn't wanted to come with him to the bullfighting at first, but he'd persuaded him. And John had loved the pure theatre of it and hadn't minded the blood at all.

Brian told me that John seduced an American tourist on holiday with her husband. The couple were celebrating their first wedding anniversary with a grand tour of Europe. The husband was a grade-one bore who spoke in an embarrassingly loud voice about how much money his stocks were earning him.

Brian was astonished because they found themselves joined by this couple as their dinner tables were rather too close. While the husband droned on, the wife, who was in her thirties and very attractive in a large, blonde American way, was almost effortlessly seduced by John without the husband noticing. When the wife made an excuse to go to the powder room, John was soon following and they were gone such a long time that Brian became concerned for the husband.

'It was obvious something had gone on when they returned to the table,' said Brian. 'John came back first and then the wife followed just afterwards looking very flushed. When they left to go to bed, I just raised my eyebrows in astonishment and John grinned. "She was a friendly girl." ' It was quite remarkable, and neither of them had even heard of the Beatles.' Brian seemed amazed that John had taken the opportunity for casual, dangerous sex when he had the lovely Cynthia at home.

John wasn't so relaxed when a disc jockey teased him about his Spanish trip at Paul's twenty-first birthday party. It was a lively afternoon occasion at Paul's aunt's house in Birkenhead and everyone was merry until John took exception to the DJ 'calling him a queer' as he described it to me afterwards. John was fairly drunk by then and he lashed out wildly at the DJ, knocking him to the ground and breaking three ribs before he was dragged off. Afterwards, he threatened legal action and we had to pay him off. I think he got £200 for an agreement to drop any claim and promise to keep quiet about the assault. There was no chance of eliciting an apology from the still furious Lennon. John told me afterwards that he thought he was asking for a good hiding so he gave him one. 'No one calls me a queer,' he said. 'And nobody bad-mouths Brian while I'm around.'

In many ways, despite his sexual preferences, Brian was rather strait-laced. In early 1962, I was approached in the shop by a couple and their very young-looking daughter who nervously asked to see Mr Epstein. Brian was in London for the whole week so I ushered them through to Brian's office. The girl was called Jennifer and she was a pretty little thing of about 16 or 17. The father spoke first.

'Well, it's like this. We don't want to bother anyone.'

The mother cut in, 'Our Jennifer is five months pregnant and the father is one of your Beatles – John,' she said emphatically.

The girl winced and I began to feel desperately sorry for her.

The mother continued, 'It's not right. She was only young when she went with him and I know it takes two but we reckon she were taken advantage of. She's going to miss out on her exams and we've no money to take care of someone else's baby. We want to see this John pays up in full for this baby's upkeep. Our Jennifer says she is determined to keep the baby and we will give it a home of course.'

I took down some notes of the conversation and promised I would report the whole thing to Brian and get back to them. Their home address was in Northenden in Manchester. I remember they did not have a phone and the mother said if she had not had a letter sorting everything out she would have to take this further. Jennifer never spoke. But as the troubled family got up to go, she handed me a small purple envelope with 'John' written on it. I took it from her and the mother glared at me as if I had personally deflowered her little daughter myself.

Brian rang in every day, and when he called that afternoon I broke the sorry story to him. He sounded very upset for the girl but he asked me, 'Do you believe them?'

I said that I did. There was an awful, lonely sadness in the girl's eyes that said more than any of the mother's angry accusations.

Two days later, he was back and we discussed the matter in detail. The Beatles were at a crucial stage in their development and Brian was clearly concerned about the threat of a scandal and the effect it might have on their budding careers. The early '60s were very different days from the liberated times that so quickly followed.

Brian arranged for the family to come back in and see him personally. He sent a car for them and we met them together. This time the mother was more subdued. Brian was very charming and he expressed enormous concern for the girl's wellbeing. He apologised on John's behalf and tried to let Jennifer down gently about the chances of renewing their relationship. Then he said, 'As the Beatles' manager, I am responsible and I have no intention of shirking my responsibilities. I think it is in everyone's interests for us to strike an agreement that takes care of the situation.'

Brian agreed to pay £250 and so much a week maintenance for the baby until it was 16. I remember that figure was to be based upon rates of payment that applied at the time. He wrote out a cheque there and then. And it was conditional upon the family keeping the baby's existence out of the newspapers. Any publicity and the whole deal was off, said Brian firmly.

Afterwards, Brian was quite upset. 'That poor young girl,' he said. 'Isn't it sad that sex always seems to have such an ugly side to it? That family could have been smashed apart by this. Do you think we have put them back together again?'

'You're sure they were telling the truth, then, Brian?' I asked. He looked shocked. He had taken every word they had said at face value and believed them completely.

'Alistair,' he said imperiously, 'I can't believe you can even think a family would put themselves through that sort of ordeal unless they were being completely honest. And not a word about all of this to John. He has enough to concentrate on. This whole affair is between you and I. The subject is now closed.'

But Brian said afterwards that what had perturbed him the most was the young girl, Jennifer. She looked a real little waif in her school uniform. Brian wondered what on earth she would have done if her parents and he had not taken charge of the situation. I said, 'Brian, some parents would have kicked her straight out of the door.'

He put his hand to his head in surprise. 'How awful!' he said, and I could see that he meant it.

My eventful association with Brian was interrupted for a few months because Lesley's asthma became so bad that the doctor advised her to live in a drier area than the misty north-west. At the same time, I was offered a good job with Pye Records and I had to move quickly. Brian was away on business in Germany so I actually explained why I had to leave to his brother Clive. When he got back to Liverpool, Brian was absolutely furious. How could I leave him in the lurch like this at such an important time? Had I no loyalty? I was shocked by his reaction. We almost had a physical fight, although I can't quite imagine Brian actually using his fists. But he was livid when he found out. He went white with anger and grabbed me and shoved me. He shouted,

'Get out. Go now. Get out of the office.' I tried to explain that I had to decide very quickly and it was for Lesley's health but he didn't want to know. He almost swore, but I don't think he did in the end. I never, ever heard him swear. He just shook me bodily.

The staff all came to find out what was going on. The shop manageress, Josie Barber, came to see what all the shouting was about. She looked stunned to see him in such a state. Brian wouldn't listen to reason and he certainly didn't want to listen to me, so I sadly picked up my coat and left. He slammed the door behind me and I was shaking with emotion by the end.

But Brian's volcanic emotions soon subsided and not long afterwards I bumped into my old boss by chance in the corridors of Pye Records. The company had signed a new Brian Epstein artist called Tommy Quigley, whose name Brian had wisely changed to Quickly. All acrimony had disappeared and Brian greeted me like an old friend. He swept me off to lunch at Bentley's and we spent the meal apologising to each other for our last encounter. Before you could say 'Top of the Pops' he had offered me a job, as General Manager of NEMS Enterprises in charge of their new London headquarters. Brian had finally outgrown Liverpool. I needed about a milli-second to consider. Brian and the Beatles were still the best act in town and Lesley and I were now happily settled in London. I started on £1,500 a year which was a good salary then.

To illustrate the sort of hard task-master that Brian Epstein was, before the meal had ended I had agreed to accompany him to his brand new flat in Whaddon House. There I was given the job of helping him to choose carpets and making sure they were ordered with underlay. My new official contract arrived at home the next day and at the bottom there was a PS, which was typical Brian. It said, 'Don't forget the underlay.'

Brian said the boys demanded that I come with him to their very next concert for a reunion. That was at the East Ham Granada. And it turned out to be a very explosive evening for me. Beatlemania was now in full flight and it was a frightening experience. The cinema was besieged by thousands of screaming, chanting youngsters. The noise was exhilarating but the pushing and shoving tested the resources of the Metropolitan Police Force to the limit.

In the dressing room, it was the usual casual chaos with Neil Aspinall struggling to control the inevitable hangers on and to protect the boys from their own astonishing popularity. Scriptwriter Alun Owen was there that night to discuss a film to be made the following summer and George Martin arrived with great news. He held up his hand for silence and announced, 'Listen, everybody. I've got something important to tell you all. I have just heard the news from EMI that the advance sales of "I Want to Hold Your Hand" have topped the million mark.'

That was the first time it had ever happened. Cheers and champagne ran round the dressing room but, as they died down, there was a mocking remark from John: 'Yeah, great. But that means it'll only be at number one for about a week.' I don't think he was joking.

The Beatles' actual performance that night was drowned out as usual by the hysteria from the audience. The boys gave it their impressive all and the crowd went collectively insane. It was a breath-taking experience from the wings. At one point, I was convinced my ears were going to burst.

The boys always closed their set with 'Twist and Shout' and I had only just heard the familiar final chords when George shouted, 'Come on, Al', and I joined in the dash to beat the fans. They grabbed me and almost bodily propelled me along corridors and down passages to the stage door which was opened for us as we sprinted. Outside, the gleaming Austin Princess limousine was there with the engine running and the doors open. In front was a police car with blue light already flashing and behind was a motor-cycle escort.

I took all this in in the flash that it took us to cross the pavement and leap into the car. Then Ringo got his foot stuck in the closing door and everyone started yelling at him. When I looked straight ahead, I realised why as hordes of fans looked on the point of breaking through the thin blue line of straining policemen. Even I started yelling at Ringo to get his foot in so we could shut the door and escape. It was only a few seconds but it seemed like ages before he freed his foot, and we sped off to the Beatles' flat in Green Street. We shot past the marauding fans just in time and hurtled through London, helped through inconvenient red traffic lights by our police escort.

We had a marvellous night when we arrived. There were just the four Beatles, Neil and myself. The Beatles rolled a joint or three and I clung to my scotch and Coke and they laughed about the early days. They took the mickey out of me for being straight, but that's me. I'm always happier in my suit than in the latest fashion item and always happier with alcohol than drugs. The boys took the piss, certainly, but in that friendly English way that let me enjoy the process. It was great to be back in the fold. It was like being a member of the best gang in the world being on the fringe of the Beatles. Apparently, you could do anything, go anywhere, and be anybody.

I realised early on in my return, however, how terribly trapped Beatlemania had made them. They couldn't go anywhere without being mobbed. There were fans camped outside their homes night and day and everything they said or did was monitored. I'd have taken drugs or any damn thing if I had to live with that pressure. Often they would almost retreat into just the four of them. They were lucky they had each other with whom to share that bizarre experience of genuine superstardom. I think being a solo version of the Beatles would send anyone round the twist, which Elvis sadly proved.

The boys used to say that their whole life was now confined to boxes. John explained it to me first in the back of a limo.

'This is one of our smaller boxes,' he joked, talking like a tour guide. 'We will live in this just for an hour or two until we are pushed into our next box which is the dressing room. We drink and prepare in there before entering a larger box, the concert hall. And next month we are touring in America which will entail squeezing into a small box called an aeroplane. Outside of all these boxes are people screaming at us. So we don't go outside the boxes.'

John was joking when he first described their lives, but they did become increasingly trapped and embattled by their spiralling fame. It always scared me and I was always delighted to be able to switch off the screams of adulation simply by leaving their company. 'Our trouble is that we can never walk away from the Beatles, so we'll have to smash them up to get away from all this nonsense,' said John darkly one night.

By the autumn of 1963, the country was firmly in the grip of Beatlemania. The Beatle Queue became a permanent feature of British life as youngsters showed they were prepared to wait for hours on end just for a chance of getting tickets to see their heroes. They arrived with transistor radios, blankets and hot water bottles and with or without their parents' blessing. The newspapers gravely recorded events across the country, as the craving to see the Beatles became a national affliction.

In Newcastle, a policewoman was kicked as fans pushed forward and ambulances dealt with more than 100 cases of fainting or exhaustion among young girls. In Hull, there were 3,000 disappointed teenagers left after 5,000 tickets had been sold and the demand usually outstripped supply by much more than that. Brian described it as the biggest thing to hit Britain since the panic to see Frank Sinatra just after the war, but I'm not quite sure how he remembered that.

The Beatles flew back in to Heathrow after a trip to Sweden and fans ran riot at the airport. There were questions in Parliament about the Beatles' fans' behaviour and one MP suggested the withdrawal of the police to see what happened. If that idiotic suggestion had been followed, the boys would have been literally torn limb from limb.

We had received an official request not to travel in the school holidays. As if Beatles' fans were not going to skive school if it meant getting a chance to see their heroes landing or taking off.

I was in charge of all the travel and found myself mainly using Pan-Am, largely because BOAC (as it then was) were so unbelievably pompous. We had to smuggle the boys in whichever way necessary to minimise the chaos but BOAC were so sniffy they didn't even like the boys going straight out to the plane. 'We only do that for MPs and bishops, not pop stars,' said one official to me, thus losing his company millions of pounds' worth of business at a stroke.

It sounds corny, but the greatest thing about my job is that the Beatles were just such fun to be with. There was never a dull moment. They had been trying to become famous and rich and successful since they were at school. When it happened, they were sure as hell going to enjoy it. John was the leader then, in spite of what everyone said about there not being a leader. He was the quickest, the strongest and the funniest. He knew exactly what he was doing when he spoke to the audience at the *Royal Variety Show*: 'The ones in the cheap seats clap your hands.' He then nodded towards the Royal Box and added, 'The rest of you, just rattle your jewellery.'

The remark brought the house down but it was never as spontaneous as it sounded. John considered several different versions of the joke beforehand but he rejected references to throwing tiaras in the air or waving your crown. As usual, his carefully chosen words were absolutely spot on. Mind you, Paul never really got the comic credit for setting the irreverent tone when they followed Sophie Tucker and he announced how delighted they were to be following their favourite American group.

The following day, the reviews were ecstatic. BEATLES ROCK THE ROYALS said the *Daily Express*. NIGHT OF TRIUMPH

FOR FOUR YOUNG MEN said the *Daily Mail*, which added underneath YES, THE ROYAL BOX WAS STOMPING. In fact, the Queen Mother had particularly enjoyed 'Twist and Shout', it was reported. And when the Queen asked where they would be appearing next, Paul told her 'Slough', only to receive the immortal deadpan reply from Her Majesty, 'Oh, that's near us.'

Marlene Dietrich was on the show and she was completely knocked out by the Beatles. She told Brian afterwards, 'It was a joy to be with them. I adore these Beatles.' Marlene was fascinated by the boys. She kept saying, 'They are so sexy. They have the girls so frantic for them they must have quite a time.'

Marlene was not wrong. The Beatles were healthy young men who liked sex as much as the next man and had rather more opportunity for multiple partners than he did. After every concert, the best-looking female fans would be given instructions as to how to get back to the hotel. It was one of the perks of the job and the boys liked their perks.

They were only in their early 20s, remember, and generally they were rampant. They had this amazing power to point and say, 'You, you, you and you,' and lovely young women would arrive at the hotel simply begging for sex. Brian's eyebrows raised in astonishment sometimes, but I think he knew he'd have been dead if he'd tried to control this particular facet of Beatle behaviour. He wasn't Machiavellian. The four guys' lives were pretty much their own.

The year of 1963 was the year the Beatles really arrived on the scene in a big way. The newspapers were way behind the public, but to be fair there had been some other huge, long-running stories, ranging from the Profumo sex scandal to the Great Train Robbery. As autumn drew on, the papers required some light relief from political upheavals and they decided to follow their readers and discover the Beatles.

Of the popular papers, who are now anxious to scream from the rooftops about every new minor pop talent, it was the *Daily Mirror* in the pompous shape of Donald Zec who weighed in first with a two-page profile headlined FOUR FRENZIED LITTLE LORD FAUNTLEROYS WHO ARE EARNING £5,000 A WEEK. He had been to a concert in Luton and then entertained the Beatles for tea in his flat.

The money was something of an exaggeration but Brian hardly minded as the coverage was long overdue. And having ignored the Beatles for so long, the papers were anxious to make up for lost stories. The *Express* had them on the front page for five consecutive days after the *Royal Variety Show*. But newspapers are difficult beasts to control and not all of the stories were what Brian wanted. It soon came out that John was not only married to Cynthia but that they had a baby son called Julian.

The second LP, *With the Beatles*, was rushed out to astonishing sales figures. Advance orders topped a quarter of a million, more than for any previously released LP. The Beatles were already making history.

Brian and the Beatles were always fun to be with in those heady early days, but I tried not to travel in a car with Brian driving too often. He was a truly terrible driver, although I never knew him to have an accident. He caused plenty, mind you. In the winter of 1964, the Beatles were playing at a huge cinema in Manchester and Brian decided he would drive the two of us over in his little maroon MGB. My heart sank. Brian announced we were going for something to eat and eventually we spotted a restaurant. Fortunately, there was a parking space just outside which would have happily accommodated an ocean-going liner. But this still represented a considerable challenge to Brian. He reversed at speed until we heard a sickening crunch from the rear. Brian grimaced and turned the radio up a notch. We lurched forward and gave the bread van in front a friendly nudge. By then, the kerb was just about within walking distance so I took the opportunity to abandon ship before Brian's manoeuvring did anyone any lasting damage. As I got out, I saw the figure of a very large policeman looming over me. At first, I thought from the tears in his eyes that he was upset about something. Then I noted from the heaving of the shoulders and the spluttering sounds that he was laughing. When Brian got out with as much dignity as he could muster, the policeman was in such a state of hysteria he couldn't find the breath to tick him off.

After our meal, we found a thick fog had fallen and we had great difficulty finding the right road to get us to the venue. Eventually, we were stopped by a mounted policeman. He leaned down to tell Brian that we couldn't go any further because a concert by the Beatles was causing widespread traffic chaos. 'Oh good,' said Brian, 'I'm their manager.'

He let us go through and we parked, this time without drama. The long queues of girls in short skirts snaked right round the cinema, much to Brian's delight. We stepped confidently past them for a quick word with the boys before the concert started. Near the lobby, we actually had to step over the prostrate bodies of girls totally overcome by the prospect of being in the presence of the Beatles. But we were stopped in our tracks by a deeply officious steward who refused to let us in. Brian explained politely who he was and the official actually used the immortal line that letting us into the building was 'more than his job was worth'. I'm afraid I lapsed into my roughest Liverpool accent and told this guy that if he didn't get out of the way instantly, then he would never work again. I think Brian was shocked, but at least a little impressed. We got in.

It wasn't long before the Beatles were due on stage so Brian and I just had a quick word to check that everything was OK. The sound of the fans was already deafening but when the boys walked on stage it was even louder.

The noise of the fans made me feel dizzy. Once the Beatles struck up the distinctive opening chords of the first song, 'Michelle' you couldn't hear a thing from them. Then I noticed that every so often, John, Paul and George would turn their backs on the audience and I realised they weren't really singing or playing a note. George came quite close to me to give the knobs on his amplifier a serious twiddling and it was clear he was not making a sound. When George wandered within a foot or so of me, I shouted, 'What are you playing at?'

'Saving our voices,' he yelled back and went off grinning widely. This unscheduled on-stage rest period lasted for about three minutes.

As General Manager of NEMS, I replaced a lovely lad called Barrie Leonard, who had been struggling in the job. At first, I was horrified that I would have to return north to Liverpool but my first job once I'd rejoined Brian was to find offices in London. I still had about five months of travelling north for the week, although Brian paid all my expenses. Initially, it was long train journeys until Brian's brother Clive suggested that taking the plane would be much quicker. I had never flown in my life before. I got a taxi from the office to Liverpool's Speke Airport to get on a terrifying World War II DC4. It was pouring with rain and we got stuck in traffic. We arrived at the airport as the plane was about to leave and a Scouse porter told me in no uncertain terms, 'Bloody run.' So I did and just caught it. We took off and almost immediately landed. I was shocked and said to another passenger, 'My, that was quick.' Nobody told me that the plane had landed to pick more people up at Hawarden just outside Chester. So much for my jet-set image.

I found a London base for NEMS Enterprises in Sutherland House in Argyll Street, appropriately next door to that bastion of showbusiness, the London Palladium. And Brian sent all staff an official letter spelling out his mission statement: 'NEMS Enterprises provides the finest and most efficient management/direction of artistes in the world.' By then, the stable of talent included The Beatles, Gerry and the Pacemakers, Billy J Kramer and The Dakotas, Cilla Black, The Fourmost, Tommy Quickly, Sounds Incorporated and The Remo Four. All of a sudden, NEMS had hit records all over the place and Brian was the hottest manager in town by a mile.

Brian always liked me to be in the office at least half-an-hour before anyone else to open all the mail and check on the running of the business. He wanted me to try to pick up any glitches before they became serious. So if anyone was writing in to complain, I would find out.

I got a shock on one of my early morning stints when I opened a slim white envelope from EMI which turned out to contain a cheque to NEMS for more than £6 million. It was for three months' royalties. The size of it was a surprise to me as Brian always kept the boys' financial details pretty close to his chest, but I couldn't believe a sum this size could simply arrive in the normal morning mail. It wasn't even a registered letter. It was a Friday and Brian was away so I took it home for the weekend for safety. On Monday, I showed the cheque and the scruffy compliments slip that accompanied it to Brian and he went absolutely bananas. He picked up the phone and rang Sir Joseph Lockwood, the Chairman of EMI, and raised the roof with his opinions of EMI business practices. A senior executive brought the next cheque round in person.

A lot of my time was spent thinking up ways to get the Beatles in and out of cinemas and theatres. The size of the crowds and the level of frenzy the fans used to get themselves worked up into were just amazing. They just used to go completely crazy. So I worked out quite a few strategies. We used decoy cars going round to the front of the building and the Beatles sneaking in at the back. And if ever there were any secret exits or little-known passageways, then we would always use those.

By the end of 1963, the Beatles had become absurdly over-exposed. Having ignored their desperate early attempts to get a foot on to the bottom rung of the ladder to success, the national Press now discovered the Beatles in a big way. You couldn't buy an issue of any paper without reading a story and seeing pictures of the group. At first, it seemed like a tremendous vindication of everything we had been trying to do. But

Brian soon became wary. He wrote in his autobiography, 'At first, the sight of the Beatles in all of the newspapers, accompanied with detailed discussion of their views, their habits, their clothes was exciting. They liked it and so did I because it was good for them and it was good for business. But, finally, it became a great anxiety. How much longer, I wondered, could they maintain public interest without rationing either their personal appearances or their newspaper coverage? In fact, by a stringent watch on their contacts with the Press and a careful and constant check on their bookings, we just averted saturation point. But it was very close, and other artists have been destroyed by this very thing.'

Brian's insight really impressed me. He always seemed to be ahead of the game. I remember he was already working out ways to reduce the level of the coverage when the boys were still desperate to be on every page of every paper. He knew the old showbiz maxim of 'leave them wanting more' and he knew that if we let the Beatles become too available, we risked cheapening the brand.

But as 1964 dawned, the Beatles became the most sought-after humans on the planet. They were distinctly working-class and proud of it, but their appeal stretched from council estates to castles. Everyone wanted to know them. They were on top of the list for invitations from every socialite worth her tiara, in demand for every charity appeal, and the must-have guests at every party. It was suddenly fashionable to be a Beatles fan. Brian and I were absolutely astonished at the reaction. We had expected acclaim and success, but this was too much for anyone, surely. Yet the boys took it all in their stride. Brian could not believe how easily they took to fame and fortune but, as we discussed it happily into the night, he considered, 'I suppose I did not realise that they wanted to succeed so much. I know they said they craved success, but I always thought I wanted it much more. It made me sick when we kept getting turned down but I see now that it must have made them even sicker.

'John and I talked in Spain about whether I would lose interest before they did. I think he thought I was some kind of playboy who would get bored with every toy he played with. I tried to explain that I was as committed as he was and he laughed at me. It was cruel but not unkind. John said rich bastards like me didn't know what it was to want to succeed. I had the family business to fall back on. He said he didn't even have a family, which I thought was a bit hard on Cynthia and his son. But John said he just wanted to show the bastards who had laughed and sneered at his dreams. He knew the music was good. He said it was the best. And he was so sure of himself and of Paul and George and Ringo. He kept saying, "We're really going to show the bastards," and I realised he was much more committed to the Beatles than I'd thought. John never liked to let you think he was taking anything seriously, but he took success seriously and he wanted a lot of it.'

THE WORLD
7

John got his wish as 1964 turned this British success story into an international pop phenomenon. And it happened quite quickly. When the Beatles went to Paris in January, they were greeted by a handful of French Press at Le Bourget airport but no fans. The journalists had been sent because their bosses had heard reports of a lot of fuss across the Channel and wanted to know if the latest British craze was worth writing about. Brian was concerned at the lack of interest in France and not all the tickets at the Olympia Theatre had been sold. But by the end of three weeks of Beatles performances, there were wailing, chanting mobs of Beatles fans laying nightly seige to the theatre and hundreds of baton-waving gendarmes were stretched to the limit to stay in control. Paris fell to the Beatle invasion and so did Copenhagen and Amsterdam.

Perhaps Brian's greatest achievement was breaking the Beatles in America. Lots of British artists had been across the Atlantic and died a death. Cliff Richard invaded the United States and nobody noticed. But Brian was determined that the Beatles would be different and he knew that timing was the absolute key.

I remember meeting him at Heathrow after one of his many early trips just after the *Royal Variety Show*. We took the car back to his house and I politely asked how it had gone.

'Oh, quite well,' said Brian quietly. 'I turned down an *Ed Sullivan Show*.'

'Brian,' I gulped, 'surely you know that *The Ed Sullivan Show* is the biggest show in America? It would be fantastic to get the boys on that.'

Brian was very cool. He said, 'Yes, I know. But we're not ready yet.'

My amazement was clearly still showing.

Brian continued, more pointedly, 'Alistair, we don't have the right record.'

He was not prepared to go over to America, use the fabulous platform of the coast-to-coast *Ed Sullivan Show*, without having the right record to back it up. I recall some time later I went into his office and he said casually, 'Oh, while you're here, listen to this,' and he had this white acetate of 'I Want to Hold Your Hand'. I thought it was a knockout and said so.

Brian smiled and sat back in his big black leather chair and said, 'Now we assault America.' That is what he wanted – a record strong enough to back it up. He was a genius of a manager, he really was. They'd had several number ones by then but he was not prepared to go to America without what he thought was the right record. He kept saying he did not want the Beatles to be another British failure in America. Brian just had this remarkable nose for knowing the right song for the right moment.

Capitol Records, the American side of EMI, could have given us a lot more encouragement to go over there a lot sooner. They didn't do us any favours. But Brian wanted to control everything – he always did. One of those myths has come up that Ed Sullivan saw the British reaction and decided to bring them over. That is not how it happened.

And, to be fair, Brian didn't always get it right. Later, he took Cilla Black over to sing in the Rainbow Room, one of the top cabaret spots in New York and she died a death. But on that occasion he didn't have a record lined up to back her up. Brian knew that 'I Want to Hold Your Hand' was the one that was going to make America sit up and listen.

* * *

So far, the Beatles hits which had been so richly appreciated in Britain had passed unnoticed in America. Traditionally, British pop stars struggled to survive the Atlantic crossing, but Brian Epstein was determined to prove that the Beatles were different. He had turned down one appearance on the *Ed Sullivan Show* but now he was ready to take on the programme that he knew could make the Beatles in the States. Sullivan, once famous for insisting that Elvis Presley be filmed only from the waist upwards, was keen to have the Beatles.

Sullivan had been on a talent-spotting trip to Europe and found first-hand evidence of the Beatles' appeal when his flight from Heathrow was delayed by fans rioting, as the Beatles flew back in from Sweden. Sullivan wanted the Beatles as a minor novelty act but Brian insisted they were to be taken seriously. He showed how serious he was by offering the Beatles at Sullivan's lowest fee so long as they received top billing. The Americans were delighted with the bargain but Brian knew what he was doing. It would have been worth mortgaging his house to pay Sullivan to let them appear. The show really was that powerful.

Thanks to a crash publicity programme which had New Yorkers waking up to 'Beatle-time on their radios', and the growing interest from kids on the streets for a chance to see and hear this group that Europe was going crazy for, the Beatles' visit to the *Ed Sullivan Show* became a major event before it even happened.

The boys were totally knocked out by the reception they got immediately on their arrival in America. Of the four of them, only George had ever even been there before to visit his sister and in those days British acts simply did not seem to work across the Atlantic. The Beatles changed all that, thanks to Brian's brilliant timing which saw the boys arrive to follow up a number-one single. What better introduction could there be than a chart-topper?

John was particularly wary. He knew that even Cliff Richard had died a death in the States and he did not want to see the Beatles embarrassed. Right up until just before departure, John was saying they were just going over to buy some LPs and take a look at the place as tourists. But the hit status of 'I Want to Hold Your Hand' changed all that.

The reception at the airport was astonishing. There were thousands of kids in Beatles wigs all screaming their heads off. Brian visibly relaxed as he saw it was going to work and the boys just had an absolute ball. The show received more than 50,000 applications for the 700 available seats to watch the filming in the studio. Even Elvis and his famously gyrating body had not generated this much interest.

The reception at the airport was sensational and the Beatles humour went down well at the introductory press conference. The boys' refusal to answer any questions seriously astonished many of the straight-faced American reporters. But when you heard the banality of the questions you could understand the boys' reactions. One ace columnist asked brightly, 'What do you do when you're cooped up in your rooms between shows?'

'We ice skate,' George deadpanned back.

John was even better. He was asked, 'Was your family in show business?' And he could not resist replying, 'Well, my dad used to say my mother was a great performer.'

Brian brought the press conference to a halt as gales of laughter started to ring round the airport. The American reporters were busy trying to describe the Beatles as the new Marx Brothers as the boys were ushered into waiting limos to be escorted by two motorcycle cops and no fewer than four New York City police cars to the unsuspecting Plaza Hotel. They had no idea who the Beatles were when they took the booking and the staff there were collectively astonished to be already besieged by fans. And this was even before they had appeared on television. Next day, 37 sacks of fanmail arrived at the Plaza.

Not everything went perfectly. George was suffering from tonsillitis and Neil Aspinall stood in for him during rehearsals for the *Ed Sullivan Show*. But George recovered after taking a variety of drugs – many of them prescribed by a doctor who was called in to get him back on his feet.

Ed Sullivan was a cynical old showbusiness pro but even he was amazed at the reaction the boys inspired. Brian decided he needed to know how the veteran host was going to present his precious stars to the American public and asked him just before recording started, 'I would like to know the exact wording of your introduction.' Sullivan did not miss a beat as he responded, 'I would like you to get lost.'

Brian was concerned, but he need not have worried. Sullivan began by reading a telegram of welcome from Elvis Presley which delighted the boys waiting to go on. They did learn much later that Elvis had no knowledge of the good luck note but by then it hardly mattered. Sullivan reported the Beatles' astonishing success in Britain to date and waved them into action with the words, 'America, judge for yourself.'

The Ed Sullivan Show on 9 February 1964 was watched by an estimated 73 million people – more than half of

America's viewers. The reviews were mixed, to say the least. The *New York Herald-Tribune* called the Beatles, '75 per cent publicity, 20 per cent haircut and 5 per cent lilting lament,' while the *Washington Post* called them, 'Asexual and homely'.

But the fans loved it. In their millions. Brian's brilliant deal to go on for a cut-price performance must have repaid itself hundreds of thousands of times over in promotional impact. It's obviously a good idea with hindsight, but in those pioneering days, no other manager would have allowed his act to go on for such a low fee. Even Billy Graham watched the Beatles, breaking a lifetime's rule not to watch TV on the Sabbath, and America's crime rate that night was the lowest in half a century.

Two days later, the Beatles gave their first live concert performance in the United States at the Washington Coliseum to scenes of extreme Beatlemania. America had fallen in love with the Beatles just as fervently as Britain. Brian told me afterwards that this was the finest single moment of his time with the Beatles. Once he knew that fans in the United States felt the same as their British counterparts he knew that we could conquer the whole world. They played a second concert on that first American trip at Carnegie Hall, the first time the famous venue had played host to a rock group, and hysteria broke out all over again.

Ringo was particularly delighted because the Americans really seemed to take to him. There was something about that laconic, hang-dog face that seemed to appeal to the Americans and suddenly he found himself headline news and in demand, even above John and Paul. 'It was a shock for me, America,' he told me. 'I loved the radio stations and the pace and energy of the place, but most of all I loved it because I wasn't just the guy at the back, the drummer.'

But it wasn't all good news conquering America. After the Washington concert, the Beatles were invited to a reception at the British Embassy and Brian decided they should go. It was a snooty affair full of the most undiplomatic diplomats imaginable. One chinless twit laughed out loud at John signing an autograph and announced loudly, 'Oh, look. He can actually write.' Surprisingly, John did not deck him, which seemed a pity to me. But he did take offence when a woman produced some scissors from her evening bag and snipped off a chunk of Ringo's hair as a souvenir for her daughter. Brian led the boys out of the party in a cold fury. He was angry that supposedly upper-class people could behave so loutishly and in the car back to the hotel he apologised to the boys and promised that they would never ever be humiliated like that again. In future, official functions were definitely not on the schedule.

The crowds were always biggest at Heathrow when we flew off on tour or returned from abroad. The worst time for me was when the Beatles returned from their first trip to America. Four of us were each assigned a Beatle to take care of and I was there to ensure John and Cynthia got through Heathrow safely. The press conference went on for so long that the fans had time to break out of the enclosure on the roof of the Queen's Building and were pushing the police cordon back at a frightening speed. They were only kids but the force of them was amazing. I saw barriers buckling under pressure as the crowd swarmed towards us. The Beatles looked really scared as the crowd got closer and we could see policemen's helmets being knocked off as the coppers started to lose control. John, Cynthia and I dived into the back of the faithful old Austin Princess. John was shaking with fear as we slammed the doors behind us and he yelled, 'For fuck's sake, get us out of here. Let's drive.' The driver sped out of Heathrow as fast as he could and we gradually started to relax. We had been told to drive along the perimeter road alongside the runway and we were followed by a frantic horde of fans. Some were running and we soon lost them but others were on motorcycles and scooters. We seemed to have the biggest tail of any of the Beatle cars, probably because the Austin Princess was pretty famous by then.

'Put your foot down and lose them,' I yelled at the driver. Well, I always did enjoy Z-Cars. And we accelerated away from most of them. We started to relax but after a few minutes the driver said, 'There is a motorcyclist following us. He has been behind from the airport.' We looked back to see this sinister lone figure all in black leathers, carefully keeping a safe distance behind. I didn't like the look of this guy at all and I ordered our driver to shake him off. The Princess lurched into a sequence of dramatic manoeuvres which succeeded only in making us all feel sick. The motorcycle was powerful and it was still on our tail.

I was concerned and I was even more worried when John said, 'Oh fuck it. Stop the car and let's see what the guy wants.' I was still trying to work out if I had the authority to countermand John's order when the car drew to a halt and he opened the door.

'Come on, mate,' he said. 'Why are you following us? Hop in the car and let's have a chat.'

The stranger took off his helmet, put his bike on its stand and stepped into the car. He had a look of amazement on his face as if he was stepping into a flying saucer. He was a bit scared but he wasn't going to miss this for the world. John pulled down the occasional seat which faced the back seats and asked him to sit down. Then they had a conversation that ranged across the Beatles, the tour, the bike, and a host of other things for several minutes. John signed his autograph and the stranger shook hands, his day made, and drove off on his bike.

John was jet-lagged from the flight, pissed off from the press conference and still shocked from the scare at the airport but he still had the ability to sit and be charming to a mysterious motorcyclist. I was horrified at the risk he had taken but John Lennon was his own man and I think he admired the bottle of the guy on the motorbike and felt he had earned himself a special one-to-one chat. For me, it was a nightmare. I was supposed to protect the guy, which is hard when he invites complete strangers into the car.

Later, we got a huge bill from Heathrow for the damage at the airport. Evidently, nine cars were badly damaged by being flattened by marauding fans. But in the end we paid nothing for the damage as it was decided we could not be held financially responsible for every fan's reaction to the Beatles.

And if we thought the pace of life with the Beatles had been lively before, it now accelerated into a blur of endless hyper-activity. Back from America, we had offers from all over the world for Beatles tours. Brian was deluged with demands to meet people, have lunch, have dinner, take holidays.

In the new headquarters next to the Palladium, Brian and I studied huge offers from Australia, South Africa, Holland, Belgium, Denmark, Finland, Israel, Hong Kong, Japan and Sweden. Arthur Howes was pressing for another British tour. The boys had just nine days off before they had to start filming their first movie, which became known as *A Hard Day's Night* once Ringo had come up with the quirky phrase. The demands on the boys to do TV and radio appearances, Press interviews, while still keeping up their output of song-writing was unbelievable and unprecedented. With the luxury of hindsight, I still marvel that they managed to maintain the quality of their work under such sustained pressure.

By the end of March, EMI announced that they had received orders of over one million copies for the new Beatles single 'Can't Buy Me Love' in Britain alone. In America, the advance orders were more than double that figure. This meant number one hits on both sides of the Atlantic. In fact, as the American fans caught up with their British counterparts in filling their record collections with Beatles songs, the sales in the United States were extraordinary. In the Billboard Hot 100 listing for 4 April 1964, the Beatles had records at numbers 1, 2, 3, 4, 5, 31, 41, 46, 58, 65, 68 and 79. And the word had spread down under as well. In Australia, the Beatles occupied the top six positions.

The pace never dropped. The Beatles finished the *Hard Day's Night* film and accompanying album and were then lined up for concerts in Denmark, Holland and Hong Kong on their way to invade Australia. They were scheduled to fly out to Copenhagen on 4 June but the day before that

Ringo collapsed at a photographic session in Barnes with tonsillitis and pharyngitis.

He was whisked straight into University College Hospital and he had been in there for less that two hours when my phone rang with a harassed hospital administrator on the line begging for advice on how to handle the avalanche of telephone calls they were getting from anxious Beatles fans. The whole business of the hospital was being interrupted because the switchboard was jammed with calls. The street outside was blocked by fans but the police were handling that and the ambulances were getting through. But it was the switchboard that had gone into meltdown. The hospital rang Brian and he smoothly handed them over to me to deal with. What was I supposed to do? But I suggested they use their medical pull with the Post Office to put some extra lines in and that's what they did.

It was a nightmare for Brian. It was much too late to cancel the tour so we somehow had to find a temporary replacement drummer. This didn't go down too well with the Beatles. George in particular refused even to consider such an idea. I don't think George's heart was ever really in the touring and he announced that if Ringo was not well enough to go, then none of them should go. George was quickly convinced that the whole tour should be cancelled. Any excuse not to go was very welcome to George and he grasped it with both hands. Fortunately, Paul, and even John, were quickly convinced by Brian that it was essential that the tour went ahead and Brian used them to convince George to get his act together. It was time to bring on the substitute and Brian and George Martin came up with drum repairer-turned-drummer Jimmy Nichol, an anonymous session musician who had played with Georgie Fame's Blue Flames. We organised a quick session that afternoon and Jimmy nervously went through six numbers with the three healthy Beatles to check him out.

Jimmy passed the audition, although I don't see how he could have failed because we really had no alternative and he joined John, Paul and George in Denmark, Holland, Hong Kong and on to Australia. The welcome there was quite extraordinary. Brian couldn't believe that there were more fans than ever and they followed every inch of the tour in their thousands. The Beatles' joint feeling of being trapped in a succession of boxes as they called it was intensified with an endless sequence of hotel rooms and concerts interrupted only by increasingly meaningless social rounds of meeting mayors and the local dignitaries. The Beatles hated it. More than 300,000 people surrounded their hotel in Adelaide hoping for a wave from the balcony. And there were crowds of over 250,000 in Melbourne. The boys were unnerved by the level of the enthusiasm. John told me he felt these huge gatherings were like the Nazi rallies in wartime Germany, which was why he would react by 'sieg heiling' to the crowd and impersonating Hitler to try to show the lunacy of it all.

It was bad enough getting Ringo to the airport on 11 June. He had recovered enough to rejoin the boys and I had to get him safely on the plane. It was my job to organise all the transport and we relied on police help a great deal. I'd fixed up for Ringo to be brought to Hounslow Police Station where I could pick him up and take him to Heathrow. Ringo is not the most organised guy at the best of times but he had me speechless half-way through the obligatory press conference. As he was in the Queen's Building fielding a sequence of mind-numbing enquiries from the ladies and gentlemen of the Press, I was asked by an official to have Ringo's passport ready, just to avoid any possible delays. I crawled down behind the table and whispered up to Ringo, 'Can I have your passport?'

He looked a bit blank and replied, 'I haven't got it, Al.'

I said, 'Stop joking around, Ringo. We haven't got much time.'

But he wasn't joking. I started to feel very hot under the collar. Travel arrangements were my responsibility and that surely included making sure the only Beatle still in the wrong country to join a world tour arrived at the airport with his passport. Ringo said it was in his suit pocket at home. Only, helpfully, he didn't know which suit. I rang Maureen and mercifully she was in. After an age she managed to find the passport but by then we were running out of time. Maureen managed to get a neighbour to rush over on his motorbike with the vital document but it still hadn't arrived when the final call for the flight went out. I turned to my friend, Whip Waterhouse, of Pan-Am, who had helped me out in so many tight corners. He breezily told Ringo to get on the plane and said to me that they'd get the passport out to him on the next flight. But by then, the world's press had sniffed out a real story in amongst the showbiz hype and they challenged Whip about Ringo's missing passport. How could he travel without it? Whip smiled and said, 'Gentlemen, a Beatle is a Beatle the world over.' As the plane took off, the door of the lounge burst open and Maureen's motorcycling neighbour rushed in, just in time to see the jet carrying Ringo and Brian take off on the first leg of its trip to Australia.

Ringo joined the boys in Melbourne on 14 June, leaving Jimmy Nichol surplus to requirements. He never seemed very happy about his brief experience with the greatest group in the world, although the boys rated him highly as a drummer. Brian gave him £500 and a gold watch inscribed to him from the boys and thought that was that. But there were rumours later that Jimmy may have thought that Brian had somehow blacklisted him after that to prevent him from ever cashing in on his fortnight of fame. I'm sure that's nonsense. Brian was not that sort of guy. He was grateful to Jimmy for getting him out of a hole.

The Australian tour was a huge success. The boys were seen by more than 200,000 people and smashed all earnings records. Even when they stopped unannounced to refuel at remote Darwin in the Northern Territory in the middle of the night, somehow several hundred fans found out about the secret stop-over and arrived to see their heroes. Remarkably, the Beatles never returned down under, but our other group on tour, Sounds Incorporated, became phenomenally popular over there and did tour after tour. They were strictly instrumental and became incredibly successful. They were pretty playful as well. I remember getting a middle of the night phone call from them accompanied by lots of squeals and giggles. They thought it would be fun to wake up Mr Fixit while actually in the act of making love to some co-operative groupies. I wasn't that prudish, but that shocked me at the time.

When the Beatles returned in triumph to London, one of the first important dates was 6 July for the charity Royal première of *A Hard Day's Night* at the London Pavilion in front of Princess Margaret. The streets around Piccadilly

Circus were closed by the police in expectation of fan trouble and more than 12,000 turned up to see the boys. My memory of that occasion was of outrage when the Rolling Stones refused to stand for the National Anthem. I suppose they thought they were making a point but they were the guests of the Beatles that night and I believe they should have shown much more respect.

I was sitting next to John Lennon and in the row behind was Mick Jagger and the rest of the Stones. They were good friends of the boys. Of course, John is seen as the great rebel but he wasn't really like that. In fact, he was first on his feet when the first bars of the National Anthem were played and all other the boys stood up. So did everyone else, except for the Rolling Stones. They sat sprawled out as an arrogant gesture of defiance. John was definitely not impressed.

The boys were much more heartened by the scale of the welcome they received back home four days later when they travelled to Liverpool for the northern première at the Odeon. It is estimated that one third of all Liverpudlians saw the Beatles that day. There were thousands of fans lining the route from Speke Airport to the civic reception at the town hall. The Beatles thoroughly enjoyed celebrating their extraordinary success with old friends.

A Hard Day's Night was just brilliant. To think that John and Paul had created those fabulous songs while immersed in the whirlwind of success amazes me to this day. It topped the charts around the world as the film showed that pop movies don't all have to be rubbish. The boys were unhappy about certain aspects but I thought it reflected some of the lunatic humour of those days. No wonder it's been success-ful all over again.

No one today has any idea of the pressure Brian put on all his artists. He worked them all very, very hard. The Beatles made stage appearances around Britain, fitted in a trip to Sweden and then went off on their first nationwide tour of the United States. Brian and I plotted 32 shows at 26 concerts in 24 cities in 34 days. If you mentioned a workload like that to one of today's bands, I reckon they would collapse with shock on the spot.

But the Beatles did it. They did not complain because this was what they had been working towards through all those long, badly-paid sessions in Hamburg. They had served their apprenticeship and earned their position at the very Toppermost of the Poppermost. But it was hard for them. Most of the time, the boys said they did not know which city they were in. Their lives became a long and bewildering sequence of aeroplanes, hotel rooms and concert halls. They started in San Francisco on 18 August and, from the moment the crowds besieged them at the airport, they almost never stopped.

At the airport they were herded into a fenced enclosure for photographs but manic pressure from fans smashed down the fences and the Beatles were whisked to safety just in time. Even worse at the Hilton Hotel, the Beatles were corralled up on the fifteenth floor, but even with the place crawling with police and security men, a middle-aged woman was beaten unconscious and robbed. Her cries went unheeded because the police thought she was just another hysterical fan.

Brian was cornered in San Francisco by a persistent American millionaire called Charles O Finlay, who was the owner of the Kansas City Athletics baseball team. Mr

Finlay was miffed that the Beatles had not included Kansas in the coast-to-coast tour of the States. And he was about to put that right. He had even announced his mission to the people of Kansas City before he'd left. Mr Finlay offered Brian $50,000 to do a single gig. When that was turned down he offered $100,000. Brian turned that down as well. Brian knew the only possible day they could fit in a Kansas concert was 17 September. But that was a precious rest day for the boys and he was not about to change it. Mr Finlay promptly wrote out a cheque for $150,000 and Brian decided it was time he talked to the boys. Brian told me afterwards he had started to warm to Charles O Finlay. He admired his single-minded determination and he quite liked his money. The Beatles were in their suite in the hotel playing another pointless card game and when Brian put the offer to them John took the lead and said, 'We'll do whatever you want.' The other three nodded in agreement. As it turned out, torrential rain helped to keep the crowd down in Kansas and Mr Finlay made a loss. It was only just over a year since the Beatles had played The Cavern.

That huge American tour was an amazing experience. The boys were constantly surprised by the excesses of America. After they had played Kansas, the hotel sold the bed linen to two Chicago businessmen who cut the sheets and pillow-cases used by the Beatles into three-inch squares and sold them on to delighted fans at $10 a time. In New York City, guys on the street were selling allegedly genuine cans of Beatle-breath and there were endless requests for used towels or even bathwater. The Beatles tried to laugh off the excesses but it wasn't always so funny, especially when disabled people were wheeled in hoping a touch from a Beatle hand would have magical healing powers.

You got used to the strangest requests from the boys, but when I got a cable from the United States asking for some of their favourite Lark cigarettes to be sent urgently to their next venue, I had to laugh. They smoked Larks in Britain, all of them. It was another illustration of their togetherness, I suppose. But I knew that Larks were American and I rang Wendy Hanson, Brian's PA, who was with them on tour, to point this out. But the answer puzzled me. Yes, they knew they were American, but the Beatles all thought that the Larks they bought in England were a lot better than the ones they got in America. So could I please send some English ones over quickly? I had learned from experience that sometimes it is better just to do as you're told, so I sent the consignment. And as I was packing up the cigarettes, I noticed on the packets that these export Larks were blended and packed in Switzerland. So they probably did taste different. So the Beatles were not quite as daft as I thought. I should have known they'd be right in the end.

Sometimes, being the Beatles resident Mr Fixit didn't seem such a great idea. Like the day George sent me a note from America. I'm not sure exactly where it was from, but then neither was he. The address was given as 'Somewhere in America' and the date as 'Sunday the something'. George told me he had seen a great picture of him in the US papers taken in an unguarded moment when he was pulling an angry face and flashing a well-known two-fingered salute. George thought this was the most hilarious photo of him ever taken. He enclosed a scrap of a newspaper with this image on and my task was to track down the original. He wanted to buy the negative, have a lifesize print made of it, and have it mounted on hardboard and have it screwed on the outside of his front door. There are a lot of photographers in America and tracking down the one who had taken this particular snap took a great deal of time and effort. But eventually a friend in Fleet Street provided a vital contact and I managed it. George was delighted with the result, but the lifesize image was so alarming he did relent enough to switch it to his bathroom door. And he had them printed on the front of his Christmas card with the seasonal greeting 'Why don't you …?' George always did have a rather individual sense of humour. George wrote, 'To Al and Lesley, without whom it would not have been possible.'

Dealing with Beatles requests was always interesting. The least demanding of the boys was Ringo. But when he did make a demand for something, it could be difficult. He came back from America hooked on the game of pool at a time when it was pretty unknown in this country. Naturally, Ringo wanted his own table for his house in Hampstead. For the weekend! I eventually found some tables in bond in Dublin. The makers were happy to supply one but it would take at least a week – until I explained it was for Ringo Starr of the Beatles. The table arrived the next day with two fitters to install it. The popularity of the boys never failed to impress me.

This was the tour that was hit by death threats and bomb scares that did nothing for the peace of mind of all concerned. George was already jumpy and now he demanded to be regularly informed of all developments to do with security. Brian humoured him with a trickle of harmless information. It wouldn't have done his paranoia any good at all to get the whole truth on what all the loonies out there were saying. Some batty astrologer predicted the Beatles' plane, chartered specially by Brian for the whole tour at a cost of just under $38,000, was going to crash en route from Philadelphia to Indianapolis with no survivors.

Fortunately she was wrong, but by the time the Beatles got back to Britain they all pledged that they would never again undertake such a punishing marathon of a tour. Even Brian privately agreed with me that for once he had perhaps pushed the boys just a shade too hard. But he barely let up for the British tour that followed in the autumn with 54 shows planned at 27 concerts in 25 towns and cities in 33 days.

As 1964 drew to a close, the Beatles had conquered the world. Their new record 'I Feel Fine' was on top of the charts and the Christmas show at the Hammersmith Odeon was a total sell-out. The Beatles had succeeded everywhere from Sydney to Sunderland and from Los Angeles to London. Nobody talked about supergroups in the days as the daft description had yet to be invented. But if they had, then Beatles would surely have been the first internationally popular supergroup.

In the early days of touring the Odeons and the Granadas, because the fans were so numerous and so enthusiastic, to get them in anywhere I had to use the police. We would arrange a meeting at a nearby police station and we would often use a police van. I remember when we played a date in Leeds we had a meeting lined up with the police at Sowerby Bridge Police Station to do the swap over. We swapped from the limo and got into the van and headed for the theatre. Suddenly, the van stopped and because there were no windows we couldn't see where we were but I didn't think we'd reached the theatre because I had already timed the route and we hadn't been driving for long enough. The doors opened and there, standing in the car park of the police station, were all the senior officers and their wives and kids waiting patiently for the Beatles to jump out and sign all their autographs and chat to their wives and kids. The Beatles were thunderstruck. Out of the side of his mouth, John said, 'Right, Al, when we get rid of this lot, we're going to sort you out.' But he was smiling as he said it. They went through the motions of signing and chatting even though they were in danger of being late for the concert and they knew that the police were way out of order hijacking their transport just so they could get to meet the Beatles. They had to be pleasant until they could get away. That happened again and again, until I could see the change gradually taking hold of the Beatles. 'I sometimes feel as if I'm public property,' Paul said to me very early on. 'I'm not a person, I'm like the Town Hall. I'm something to be stared at and it seems like I always have to be open.' The boys resented the police abusing their position.

Little did I realise at the start of the '60s just what an era was beginning. I believe the Beatles' arrival heralded all sorts of changes, in the recording industry and in society at large. Entire lifestyles changed for ever in fashion and in attitudes and I believe the Beatles were an immense force for change.

In the beginning, there was an enormous furore over their hair. And yet if you look at the early pictures of the Beatles after Brian's total makeover of suits and haircuts, they just look so smart. It's incredible to think that they sparked a

On yer bike! John Lennon cadges a ciggie from me during the filming of *Magical Mystery Tour* and, (*inset*) John puts his feet up for a rest, while I take a break in the background.

NEMS ENTERPRISES LTD

SUTHERLAND HOUSE, 5/6 ARGYLL STREET, LONDON, W.1
TELEPHONE: REGENT 3261

[signature]

Welcome to the new offices.

Attached is a copy of a letter which is being sent out to all artistes.
I hope you will note its most important message: "that Nems
Enterprises provides the finest and most efficient management/direction
of artistes in the world". This must be without question our principal
aim and should be borne in mind by all staff.

Alistair Taylor will be advising you of the details of operating the
new offices, but I would like personally to point out one or two things.

First of all as our organisation is very much in the public eye, it is
most important that we present the best possible "front". By this I
mean that all visitors must be treated with utmost courtesy. That
work must be carried out smoothly and efficiently without fuss. And
most important, that the offices themselves must be kept tidy and clean
at all times.

Another matter which I must ask you to treat with considerable care
is the question of divulging to unauthorised or persons outside the
organisation information concerning the company. It is strictly out
of order for anyone to discuss with the press any business (however
slight or remotely connected) whatsoever. Your adherence to this
ruling is of great importance.

I really hope that you will be happy and as comfortable as possible in
our new surroundings.

With best wishes for the future. *[signature]*

P.S. If there should be anything which you may wish to discuss with me,
please do not hesitate to ask my assistant Eileen Lewis for an appointment -
she will arrange it quickly. I would like you to know that the general
welfare of personnel within the organisation is of the utmost importance to me.

My original contract and
welcome letter for my job
with NEMS Enterprises,
signed by Brian Epstein.

Service Agreement dated .... 29th January, 1965.

between

NEMS ENTERPRISES LTD.,
23 ALBEMARLE STREET,
LONDON, W.1.   ("the Company")

and

JAMES ALISTAIR TAYLOR

("the Employee")

The Company engages the Employee and the Employee agrees to serve the Company as ....
GENERAL MANAGER
....on the following terms and conditions:—

1. **TERM:** **1 YEAR, 9 MONTHS** ~~YEARS~~ from the date of this agreement. Unless then terminated by the Company
by thirty days written notice the engagement shall continue thereafter subject to termination by either
party at any time on thirty days notice.

2. **SALARY:** £ **550** per annum payable monthly at the end of each calendar month.

3. **HOLIDAYS: THREE** weeks per year with full pay at such times as may be convenient to both
parties.

4. **ABSENCE** caused by illness, etc: The Company may determine this agreement without notice if
through illness or other justifiable cause the Employee is absent from his duties for an aggregate of
six weeks in any fifty-two consecutive weeks. Until such determination the Employee shall be paid full
salary for the first four weeks' absence and fifty per cent of salary thereafter. The Employee shall not
be required to account for any monies received under the National Insurance Act, 1946 in respect of
illness.

In case of illness a doctor's certificate shall be produced to the Company in respect of any absence of
more than two days duration.

5. **DISMISSAL** for breach of regulations, etc: The Company may at all times dismiss the Employee
without notice on grounds of breach of the Company's regulations or other improper conduct.

6. **GENERAL TERMS**

   a) The Employee shall comply with all reasonable and proper instructions and directions of the
   Company and attend punctually at such places as his duties may require and devote his whole
   time and attention to the business of the Company during the Company's usual business hours.

   b) The Employee will not during the continuance of his employment by the Company be concerned
   in any manner whatsoever with any other business similar to that of the Company unless any
   such business activity has been specifically authorized by the Company.

   c) The Employee will not divulge to any person or persons during or after the period of this
   engagement any information coming to his knowledge during this engagement concerning the
   Company's business or clients or communicate with (except on the Company's business) or solicit
   any clients of the Company.

Signed For and on Behalf of the Company

[signature]

DIRECTOR

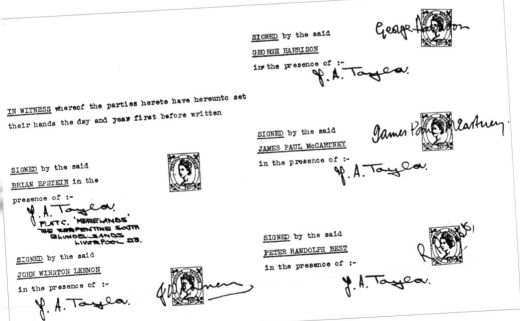

Above: The Beatles performing at the Cavern Club in the early days, with Pete Best behind the drum kit. When Brian and I first saw them at the Cavern, we were dazzled by their raw talent and charisma.

Below: A piece of history, and I witnessed it in the making! The first contract between Brian and the Beatles – I signed for Brian. He said he would add his signature later, but never did!

NEMS ENTERPRISES LTD

DIRECTORS: B. AND C. J. EPSTEIN

PRESS OFFICE : 13, MONMOUTH STREET, LONDON W.C.2. TELEPHONE COVent Gdn 2332

Monday 2 March 1964

CHANGE OF ADDRESS

This month Brian Epstein moves his company offices from Liverpool to London. With effect from the morning of

MONDAY 9 MARCH 1964

the new address for NEMS ENTERPRISES LTD and NEMS PRESENTATIONS LTD, previously located in Liverpool will be **SUTHERLAND HOUSE (5th FLOOR) 5/6 ARGYLL STREET LONDON W.1.**

The suite at Sutherland House will include the PRESS AND PUBLICITY DEPARTMENTS previously located in Monmouth Street.

For All Departments Please Telephone REGent 3261

J. ALISTAIR TAYLOR
General Manager
(Home telephone: KELvin 7345).

J. B. MONTGOMERY
Accounts.

TONY BARROW
Press and Public Relations Officer
(Home telepnone: REDpost 2735).

BRIAN SOMERVILLE
Beatles' Personal Press Representative
(Home telephone: STReatham 3987).

WENDY HANSON
Personal Assistant to Brian Epstein.

The following artists are under the sole direction of Brian Epstein:-

THE BEATLES ::: GERRY AND THE PACEMAKERS ::: BILLY J. KRAMER
THE DAKOTAS ::: CILLA BLACK ::: THE FOURMOST ::: TOMMY QUICKLY
SOUNDS INCORPORATED ::: THE REMO FOUR

With Compliments from

Tony Barrow

Press & Public Relations Officer

With success came change: this notice announces the management move from Liverpool to London.

The smart and astute Brian Epstein, captured at the Cavern Club.

Above: On the road to success: the boys just after they had released their first record, 'Love Me Do', pictured here in Carlisle. The record peaked at no. 17 in the charts, in December 1962.

Below: Brian had a punishing promotional schedule for the boys, including many television appearances. Here, John and Paul are pictured with Brian recording a TV show in Blackpool.

En route to Athens. John and son Julian lead the way, followed by myself and Cynthia, with Paul and Jane Asher behind us.

Paul with one-time girlfriend Jane Asher. The two were inseparable for years and after their split, Paul married Linda.

John with first wife Cynthia. When Cynthia gave birth to their son, Julian, John had to wear a disguise to visit them in hospital.

The real fifth Beatle?!

Above: Limbering up for the Royal Variety performance in 1963. It was during their performance at this show that John brought the house down with his jokes.

Below: Meeting Princess Margaret – and perhaps putting in a word for their MBEs!

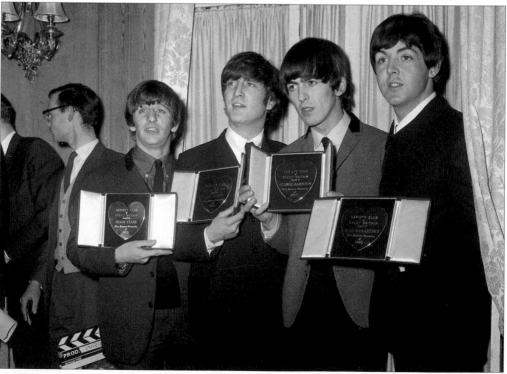

By now the Beatles really were 'toppermost of the poppermost'. *Above*, the hysteria as Beatlemania gets into full swing and, *below*, proudly displaying their Variety Club Awards.

Brian knew that, despite their fame in Britain, the Beatles had to break into the USA.
Brian accepted the lowest ever fee to get them top billing on the Ed Sullivan Show.

Beatles in love. *Above*: George weds the beautiful Pattie Boyd and, *below*, Ringo ties the knot with Maureen Cox.

We managed many names besides The Beatles, including Cilla Black. Here I am watching one of her performances, having just had to convince her boyfriend that she was not having an affair with Adam Faith!

Your's truly: the band's Mr Fix-It. Whatever they needed, I would make sure they got it!

storm and were known as the 'Moptops' in those early days, because of their long hair. It was absolutely nothing. Brian used to have each set of sheet music framed and put up in the corridor on the way to his office and, as the years went by, we used to have great giggles because you could see that in those early days with 'Please, Please Me', their hair seemed positively short. It was only as they moved on towards Sergeant Pepper, their hair was down over their shoulders and you could see their history through the Beatle hair.

Before any gig, it became a habit for children in wheel-chairs to be brought in and sort of presented to them. It was very sweet and at the start they meant it most sincerely. But the frightening thing was that parents began to believe that if one of the Beatles touched their child then he or she would be healed. This soon became quite a sick practice. It turned my stomach and I didn't like it. They received a lot of credit for allowing disabled children into their dressing room. Neil Aspinall would line it all up. He would check up the corridor to see if they were all waiting then he would come inside the dressing room and, mimicking John's humour and purely to get the Beatles' attention he'd shout, 'OK, guys, spastic time.' They and Neil felt very uncomfortable about all this. They used their black humour to disguise their real feelings but Paul told me how much he hated the way people used to use crippled or handicapped children to get backstage.

'It started out innocently enough,' he said. 'These kids have mostly had such a shit deal from life they deserve the best seats in the house. That's fine, but it never stops there. They want to come into the dressing room, to meet us before the show, and they start to think we've got healing hands or something. We don't want to do a damn thing to hurt any kid, sick or otherwise. That includes John. He might make some sicko jokes but when it comes down to it he's about the softest guy I know about any sort of suffering. But if there's any hint of us not co-operating, then we get threats of guys going to the papers. It's just cruel to tell kids that touching a Beatle will make them better.'

The big time had arrived by now but we still seemed haunted by memories of the old days. We did an appearance for BBC Manchester and the payment was so pathetic it didn't even cover the fares from Liverpool to Manchester. Brian ordered me to get on the telephone to the BBC and demand more money. We couldn't possibly operate at a loss. I could see Brian's point but it was still a hell of an embarrassing conversation.

One of Brian's finer qualities was that he never forgot the people who had helped him on the way up. Louis Buckley was an old promoter out at Southport who used to always book the Beatles for about £12 a time. And when they made it to the big time, Brian gave him at least three dates when they could have charged much more for that same £12. It was a thank-you for him supporting them when they needed it.

The Beatles worked incredibly hard on their music. They always seemed to prefer to work at night. And they used to go on long into the night. I remember that my eyelids would be drooping in the early hours at Studio Two at Abbey Road when they were still very hard at work. They would just keep on and on. That way, ideas seemed to keep coming. Of course, John and Paul emerged as the driving force but the part played by George and Ringo is too often forgotten or played down. Their contribution was highly significant as the boys insisted on putting layer on layer on layer to get exactly the sound they wanted. They seemed to draw energy from the actual music.

By 2.00am I would be exhausted and dying to go home and they would be trying something new. All four of them were totally into music and what they were creating. It wasn't that they were the Beatles and this had to be great. The mood was more like 'That's a great song, let's get it down.' They were really turned on by their music.

Often, I remember one of the boys shouting up at George Martin and asking if they could do another version. You could see from the expression on George's tired face that he thought they had already got it but he would say 'Yes' with all the enthusiasm he could muster. And even though there was nothing wrong with the last version, somehow they would manage to improve upon it. That happened time and time again. And George would smile in admiration. George was astonished at how it all worked out. In the beginning, he was ordered at least to give the Beatles a try. He never knew what he was taking on. If the potential of the Beatles had been recognised at the start, they would definitely have gone to one of the main pop music producers.

John and Paul, as well as being the driving force of the group in those exciting early days, were the firmest of friends. People who talk about early conflicts are mainly talking crap. Sure, they had their moments, but to me it looked like John and Paul leading George and Ringo against the rest of the world. And it's Lennon who has become the most misunderstood. I'm not saying he was a saint but to me he was a hell of a nice guy. He has been signed off as being the hard man, and cruel to women, brutal to Brian. But he could be so gentle. He was a sardonic bastard. I think he was the biggest piss-taker the world has ever known.

But there was a gentle side to John. On one of the very rare occasions my wife Lesley came to see a concert, I remember we were in the dressing room at the Streatham Odeon before the show. The room was heaving with people and the boys were in a huddle in one corner having something approaching an argument about something musical. All of a sudden, Lennon's powerful voice rose above the rest: 'GET FUCKED.' Then everything went quiet. And John's head slowly emerged from the crowd.

'Sorry, Lesley, I got a bit carried away.' That was John Lennon, the wild man of rock, apologising for swearing, embarrassment showing on his red face.

John Lennon was a special guy and I suppose I always felt the most protective of him. Not that he needed anyone's protection, of course, it was just that because he was so upfront and outspoken I always wanted to go after him explaining to people that he'd only been joking and that he was a really nice bloke underneath. Somehow he was more vulnerable than the others because he did wear his heart on his sleeve sometimes. He needed looking after.

John Lennon was in the office once and I was getting the documents together for their trip to the United States. I saw that John's passport had had the photo ripped out of it. I started to tease him about it saying, 'That's a bit daft, Lennon. Even you have to have your photo in your passport.'

He said, 'Well, I hated it. It was a horrible photograph. Get me a new one.'

I tried to explain you couldn't just stick a new one in. 'Oh you can do it, Mr Fixit,' he laughed. I went down to Petty France in London and tried to explain my problem to an official. I told him the photo had fallen off. He explained that it could not do that because it was such strong glue. I had to admit John had ripped it out and threw myself on his mercy. He agreed, considering who it was, but he insisted I tell Mr Lennon not to be a stupid boy again.

Working for Brian was certainly never boring. One of my most bizarre tasks was to help organise a wedding for a German guitarist.

Klaus Voorman was a German guy the Beatles first met up with in the early days in Hamburg. He was a lovely guy, a good guitarist and a talented artist, and had drawn the *Revolver* cover. When I first met up with him, he was with a band called Paddy, Klaus and Gibson. Brian wanted to sign them up and work with them in this country which was a problem at the time because Klaus was German and the Home Office were being sticky about issuing him with a work permit.

But then he married *Coronation Street* actress Christine Hargreaves and Klaus Voorman. It was a very sudden wedding, and they are a great couple; it also meant that he could so that he could stay in this country and work as a musician. When I saw him years later, I was pleased that Klaus recognised me as I had worked to organize his wedding. Brian kept in touch with Christine, who sadly died young only a few years later.

THE ESCAPES
8

Paul met Jane Asher in 1963 when she came to write a piece for *Radio Times* magazine on the Beatles appearance at the Royal Albert Hall. All four of them took a shine to Jane, as did most of the males in the Royal Albert Hall. She was delightful. When they first met her, the boys couldn't get over her lovely red hair. They'd thought she was blonde because they had only seen her on black-and-white telly on shows like *Juke Box Jury*.

Gradually, I became closer to Paul than to any of the others. When he was going out with Jane, we were very close. He came to the office one day and told me that he had bought a farm in Scotland. He had had it for about four years and not done anything about it, let alone seen it. He asked me to go up and take a look to see where he could build a new farmhouse. I went up there on the overnight train and tramped around and discovered that the Scots had already built a house on the only suitable spot but the existing building was just about derelict. The farm hadn't been lived in for five years. There were 400 acres of nothing but sheep and wind. I couldn't understand how the poor creatures managed to stay upright in those endless gales. There was hardly anything inside the house except a very low toilet. Perhaps you'd be blown off a high one.

For Paul to build a new home up there, I said to him that he'd have to knock the old one down and build on the plot. He said the photos looked great, in fact 'Really groovy' were the words he used. He asked me to get some furniture, but everything had to be second-hand and old, except for the beds. 'I want it to be really basic and Spartan,' said Paul, who always had an affection for life at its most primitive. He was absolutely sick of luxury and wanted to get right back to basics. So I organised him a Formica table, three plastic dining chairs and a second-hand electric stove. He did insist on clean bedding, though, and there was no bath.

The three of us went up there. Paul, Jane and I flew to Macrihanish, which I discovered was a NATO airbase. It was run by the RAF so I rang the commanding officer and when I asked about the chances of landing a private plane there he said, 'You have got to be kidding.' That was one of the few times I used the Beatles fame. Mostly, I tried to keep them out of everything but I couldn't see any other way of getting permission. I said actually it's for Paul McCartney and, miraculously, permission was granted. When we landed for the first time all the staff were there. Paul signed autographs and chatted and went into the Mess. The base only consisted of two big runways off to the Atlantic, where I'd arranged for John, the local taxi driver, to pick us up. The road to the farm became more and more rugged and I could tell that they were becoming really excited at the thought of being able to walk outside without being mobbed by crowds of teenage girls. I was still a little apprehensive about what they might think of the place. It was very remote and basic and very cold. Lots of people are drawn to the idea of getting away from it all, but sometimes the reality is a little too rough to handle. But Paul and Jane fell in love with the place at first sight.

High Park seems to stand up in defiance of all the elements. Paul and Jane marvelled at the complete absence of luxury and even everyday modern conveniences. They spent the first hour there exploring and wandering around the farm and its tumbledown buildings. They kept squealing out in delight to each other when they found an old washtub or a piece of dead tractor. I never knew junk could be so interesting, but you could see this was exactly the escape they had both dreamed of. The farm hadn't been used for years and there were piles of old bits of machinery lying around. The sheep that we saw grazing belonged to Paul, but they were looked after by High Park's neighbour Ian, who lived at the rather more hospitable Low Park.

That evening, he paid us a call. Paul welcomed in this cheery chap with a weather-beaten face and an accent so strong that the three of us dared not look at each other for fear of offending our visitor with laughter. We kept nodding and saying 'Yeah' or 'No' in the hope that we would be able to penetrate his accent. Jane had to leave the room to stifle her giggles as Paul and I studied Ian's face intently to see if we could comprehend at least the odd word. Eventually Paul gave in and said, 'Ian, I'm sorry, but I can't understand a word you're saying.' We all burst out laughing and Ian laughed the loudest of all. Jane came back from the other room still sobbing with mirth and Ian slowed down and straightened up his speech just enough for we foreign invaders to understand. He was kindness itself as he carefully advised us where to walk and where not to walk and promised that he and his housekeeper Isobel would be around if we needed any help.

We needed something to sit on. We wandered into the barn and up in the rafters was a filthy old mattress and piles and piles of old potato boxes, which had previously held Sharp's Express potatoes. Paul said, 'Let's get that down. The mattress can be our sofa. We'll have to give it a good beating to get the dust out. We can build the frame from the boxes.'

I was despatched into Cambeltown by taxi to buy a big bag of nails and a couple of hammers for this millionaire Beatle to start making furniture from the basic raw materials. 'Get as many felt pens as you can as well because we're going to doodle all over these horrible chocolate-brown walls.'

We hammered old boxes into the shape of the sofa base and then crudely hammered on a back. We threw the still filthy mattress on top and lo and behold we had our sofa. Paul instantly christened it our 'Sharp's Express'. But we didn't stop there. The spirit of Chippendale and Hepplewhite entered us and we made some cupboards to stand beside the beds and some more for under the kitchen sink, all out of boxes. The next time I went into town, I bought some paint for all the cupboards, but tastefully leaving our Sharp's Express sofa as raw wood.

There were no carpets, just bare stone floors. Paul used to have endless battles with the elderly Aga that simply refused to light until he had been fiddling with it for several hours. Even when he got it going, it sent smoke billowing all over the kitchen. But Paul liked the atmosphere it produced so he insisted we always kept it burning. Jane cooked our meals on a horrible old electric cooker which we had picked up for virtually nothing. She was a super cook and you would never tell from the meals she served up what a basic kitchen she was working in. But they were both fervent vegetarians and sometimes it seemed that all we lived on was cauliflower cheese.

After a day or two, we decided we all needed a bath. We were determined to solve our own problems rather than sneak off to Ian's house for home comforts. So we decided to use the big old milk tank that stood in the derelict dairy. It was a huge stainless steel tank that stood on a plinth. It was about three feet deep and Paul said, 'I've got it. We'll rig this up as a bath. All we need is a stepladder!' The immersion heaters warmed up the water and we filled our enormous bath. We found a stepladder and took turns to go up into our bath. When you were inside you couldn't see out but getting in was not exactly dignified. There was no one for miles around to see you but in those old-fashioned days Paul and I stood on guard against intruders with our backs to the bath when it was Jane's turn to get inside. Well, I had my back to the bath anyway. It was a great place for a good old splash and a soak.

Mind you, Paul was not always quite as squeaky clean as he would have liked Jane to believe. He and I had taken Martha (Paul's great, daft Old English sheepdog) for a walk in the fields and he turned to me and said, 'You'll have to go to the chemists in Cambeltown for me, mate. I've got an itch. I hope it's not crabs. Get me something quick. I don't want Jane to find out.'

Goodness knows who'd given him the crabs or whether he ever even had them. I suspect it was his paranoia, because he loved Jane and hadn't strayed. Even being in love didn't stop a Beatle from straying from the straight and narrow in those days. In the end, I had to get our solicitor Bob Graham to help me out. I phoned and told him it was for me and he said, 'OK, mate, I'll make sure some comes up.' I'm pretty sure he knew it was for Paul because I had to stress secrecy. Eventually some pills arrived labelled 'Sheep Dip', so that Jane would not find out.

There was a simplicity and an innocence about High Park in those early visits that impressed even an old cynic like me.

There were round-the-clock pressures involved in being a Beatle and High Park was a wonderful escape. Jane was famous in her own right as well, of course, and she loved the feeling of freedom that the isolation gave them. At the risk of sounding unbearably corny, I can't recall ever seeing a young couple happier. It was a privilege to be around such a happy, generous pair. Mind you, they weren't alone for long as Martha also loved life at High Park. The first time Paul suggested bringing her along, I was horrified. I said, 'Paul, Martha has never been in a plane in her life. If she goes berserk on a small private plane, we're in trouble.'

'Don't be a drag, Al,' said Paul, 'she'll be all right.'

So off we set, the three of us and Martha. And she just sat there in the plane, bless her. She was as good as gold.

She might have been a city dog, born and bred in St John's Wood, but she loved the wide open space and even tried to round up the sheep for dipping with a singular lack of success, as she finished up much more exhausted than the sheep although she did chase one sheep into a hedge.

I enjoyed many visits with Paul and Jane. Sometimes we would go and help Ian with his sheep, and at other times we'd just wander at random on the unspoilt acres. It was so remote and peaceful it was the perfect remedy from an attack of Beatlemania. There was even a huge stone, which was later used as a title for a classical piece of music called 'Standing Stone'.

There was a little lake on Paul's Scottish estate with a rowing boat tided up at the edge. One day, we decided on a boating trip and the three of us climbed in. Paul took the oars and we started to float slowly round. I dangled my hand in the water as I relaxed in the sunshine and caught hold of a weed. I pulled this waterlily plant out by its roots and I was just about to hurl it casually back when Jane suddenly launched into a fierce lecture. 'Do you know that plants are living creatures and that you have just killed one?' she screamed at me.

None of the other Beatles ever went there. I felt very close to Paul at this time. High Park was very special to him. It was a super-magical place. Once, we heard shotgun blasts. It turned out to be Ian warning off the junior reporter from the local paper. He had spotted him approaching the farm and let loose a couple of cartridges, mercifully well over his head. The poor lad had turned tail and run, apparently unprepared to dodge gunfire for a story. Paul felt so sorry for him afterwards that he gave him an exclusive interview.

Jane seemed to be the first woman that Paul took seriously. Until Jane, women were there to be had. They were just throwing themselves at the Beatles in those days. What healthy young man would not take advantage? Girls used to queue up for the chance of going to bed with the Beatles. Sex was so frequent and so bereft of any emotion that it became boring.

John Lennon said to me, 'When I was a kid, I wanted to shag every attractive woman I saw. I used to dream that it would be great if you could just click your fingers and they would strip off and be ready for me. I would spend most of my teenage years fantasising about having this kind of power over women. The weird thing is, when the fantasies came true they were not nearly so much fun. One of my most frequent dreams was seducing two girls together, or even a mother and daughter. That happened in Hamburg a couple of times and the first time it was sensational. The second time it got to feel like I was giving a performance. You know how when you make love to a woman that the moment you come, you get a buzz of relief and just for a moment you don't need anyone or anything. The more women I had, the more that buzz would turn into a horrible feeling of rejection and revulsion at what I'd been doing. As soon as I'd been with a woman, I wanted to get the hell out.'

The one woman John Lennon was most keen to bed was the French film star Brigitte Bardot. She had been a persistent fantasy figure for all the boys but Lennon being Lennon could not resist attempting to make his fantasy come true. He got Derek Taylor to organise a meeting with Brigitte when she was staying in London. She was interested in the idea and a date was fixed at her Mayfair hotel. But John was really nervous about the whole thing and decided unwisely to increase his confidence with a mixture of drugs and alcohol. He was completely out of his brain by the time he got into Brigitte's room and by his own account totally incapable of rising to the occasion. The French sex symbol was apparently very let down by the whole incident and John was ribbed mercilessly by the other Beatles for weeks. John was inconsolable afterwards. He told me, 'I'd been thinking about shagging Brigitte Bardot ever since I was at school. One of the first thoughts I ever had about Cyn was that she looked a bit like her. But when it came to it, I was ridiculously nervous. Getting the chance to shag a woman you wanked over for years does strange things. She was keen enough and we played around a bit but when I needed my biggest erection there was just ... nothing. Very embarrassing. I tried to tell her it was nothing personal but what could be more personal than that?'

Brian could see the potential for disastrous publicity if details of lots of illicit sex hit the papers. They had an image to keep up. But it could be done quietly and covertly.

Brian's way was the wholesome image. While The Who were wrecking hotel rooms and smashing things up, we never ever had any of our groups refused accommodation by a hotel. I did all the hotel booking and we never had a problem like that. They didn't flaunt the fact that they'd had a stream of groupies in their rooms. But, boy, the Beatles could party. It's just that Brian kept such a tight control on the Press. He had most of the writers in his pocket because there was such a flow of stories coming from his stable of artists that it would have been suicidal for any writer to start stirring up trouble.

The Beatles hated filming *Help!* early in 1965. All the endless hanging around waiting for a couple of minutes' work bored them to tears. *A Hard Day's Night* had been fun because it was the first and they did not know what to expect, but by the time *Help!*, the second of the three-film deal, came around, they knew that this was a directors' medium which involved a lot of waiting for everyone else. It was at this point that they decided 'Never again', and that's why the third film, *Yellow Submarine*, became animated. The Beatles had lost patience. As John put it one night, 'Fuck off. We're not going through that again.' But on the bright side, they brought out *Rubber Soul*, which I thought was a great album.

THE PALACE
9

It was June 1965, and it was obvious that Brian had something special to tell me when he discreetly phoned me at home after work. Could I possibly pop over to his house to discuss something rather delicate? When I arrived, he offered me a drink and then lowered his voice as if the whole place might possibly be bugged. He had just heard from Buckingham Palace that the Beatles were to be awarded MBEs and he was anxious about security.

'Alistair, we have to make sure that the Beatles get in and out of Buckingham Palace safely on the day of the ceremony. We can't have any mistakes or incidents which might embarrass the Queen. Will you liaise with the Palace and make sure that all the arrangements are absolutely watertight?'

My heart skipped a beat. Had I heard correctly? Was I, a former humble timber importer's clerk from the wrong side of Runcorn really being asked to liaise on security with Buckingham Palace? The responsibility was awesome.

It's fair to say that the announcement that the Beatles were to receive the MBE did not inspire universal applause. There were widespread protests from various quarters against four long-haired singers and musicians being given this great honour. Several members of the House of Lords woke up for long enough to deliver angry condemnation. Previous recipients of the medal sent theirs back in disgust and a retired colonel exploded with anger, claiming that he was not going to give the Labour Party his £11,000 bequest after all, or his collection of military medals.

The Beatles weren't all very keen on the idea either. Ringo was delighted at the prospect at 'getting a badge' from the Queen, as he put it. John regarded it as one of the many sell-outs he had been required to undergo as the price of being a Beatle. He said they agreed it was daft and that they thought about turning it down. But there was a lot of pressure from their families and also from Brian who was ecstatic at the accolade. I thought Brian should have got one as well because they were given to recognise the Beatles' services to British exports and, without Brian, there's a pretty good chance that they would have never exported a bean. One of the saddest aspects of the whole event was that Brian was not even invited to the Palace.

When I telephoned the Palace, I was put through to the head of the Buckingham Palace constabulary. I didn't even know the place had its own police force. But I was invited down to discuss the security implications and, I have to admit, it was a task that thrilled and terrified me at the same time.

The best bit of the whole day was getting into a car and telling the driver, 'Buckingham Palace, please.' By the time I arrived, I had calmed down a little and realised that I had better take this pretty seriously. The top cop gave me a lesson in planning and expecting the unexpected. We would only have done our job correctly if there were no unforeseen incidents. He saw no major problem, but then he didn't know the Beatles and he had had no experience of their capacity for clowning around, especially when confronted by representatives of an Establishment they did not have a great deal of respect for. And I was thinking of the anarchic Mr John Winston Lennon in particular. The combination of the Queen and the Beatles was about as big a draw as it gets in this country and very possibly in the whole world. Nothing must go wrong.

In summer 1965, the Beatles headed off on a brief tour of Europe but audiences in France, Italy and Spain were disappointing. The normal sell-out success was missing and Brian was concerned that fans were tiring of the Beatles. But the Beatles were put in such huge venues it was hardly surprising. Sophisticated Italians were not impressed with the prospect of seeing the Beatles from 400 yards away in enormous football stadiums and I know the Beatles longed for the intimate Cavern dates where they could establish a real rapport with their audience. George told me angrily, 'They could stick four puppets in the distance and produce the same effect. Or maybe that's what they are already doing.' He felt more and more manipulated by the Beatles machine that ground relentlessly on.

Brian had flown to America at the start of the year to tie up another big summer US tour where the Beatles' popularity was showing no signs of declining. He had lined up some enormous venues. It opened at Shea Stadium in New York in front of more than 55,000 fans. The Beatles could always rise to the big occasion and this was one of the great Beatles nights. But the old enthusiasm was ebbing away. John would cheerfully yell 'Shut up' at fans and the Beatles knew that the crowd were making so much noise it didn't really matter how they played. Indeed, to illustrate the pointlessness of their performances, they took to taking long breaks from actually producing any sound and no one seemed to notice.

American fans seemed the most determined to get at their idols. In Houston, some 5,000 fans broke down the security fences and surrounded the plane. To get them off, the police had to mount a hostage-style operation springing the Fab Four into a security van from the emergency exit. The

Beatles were insured for $5.5 million each at Lloyd's of London and when they finally flew home on 1 September 1965, they were $1 million richer.

But they had had enough. John told me over a drink, 'If Brian thinks we're spending the rest of our lives living like this, he can fucking think again.' To Brian's face, the Beatles insisted the touring was going to have to stop. We had lined up a British tour for the autumn and winter but the Beatles said they wouldn't do it. And they firmly ruled out doing another Royal Command Performance.

This was the first major rebellion by the group against Brian's leadership and I know it hit him hard. In his heart, he knew they were talking sense. Only a maniac would have wanted to carry on living the sort of life they had, but in his head he had put together a lucrative string of live appearances. There was a real battle behind the scenes and, typically, I could see both sides of the argument. In the end, common sense and a great British compromise prevailed. The Beatles would do a nine-concert tour.

But before then, the Beatles were to receive their Membership of the Excellent Order of the British Empire at Buckingham Palace on 26 October. We had planned it like a military operation. The policeman at the Palace explained that on Investiture days it was the custom for all those arriving to be honoured to queue in their cars along the Mall, slowly filtering into the Palace forecourt. I was horrified. The idea of the Beatles waiting in a queue of cars in central London was out of the question. The vehicle would be mobbed and would probably arrive in the Palace with a couple of hundred teenage girls clinging to the roof. Our plan was that the boys' car would drive round the back of the Palace from Victoria.

This way, the fans didn't get a sight of them sitting in a traffic jam, and the car would enter through the open gate just to the left of the main gate, which would then be smartly slammed shut preventing anyone from following them inside. Fortunately for my reputation as Mr Fixit, the plan worked like a dream. But inside the Palace was another story.

The lads were so determined to be cool about the whole experience that they'd never admit it, but in fact I've never seen them so nervous. John was deeply impressed by the beauty of the Palace and he loved having flunkeys to open the door for him. But he knew the perfect way to relax his nerves, and that was by smoking a joint in the Buckingham Palace toilets. The others joined in, according to John and, in fact, by the time they came to meet the Queen, they were giggling and on the way to being out of their heads. Presumably, her Majesty put the mirth down to nerves. George later insisted that they had only smoked cigarettes but John admitted to me that they had all smoked reefers.

In fact, John also had a couple of tabs of acid with him. He told me just afterwards that he had planned to slip it into the Queen's tea just to liven up proceedings. He seemed serious but with John it was always hard to tell. He said it would be a blast if he could make the Queen feel as if she was flying and he was determined to sneak the tab into whatever she was drinking. 'I want to open her mind and try and get her to declare war on somewhere nice and warm so we can all go and fight on the beaches. Or perhaps she'll set free everyone in prison and send Harold Wilson to the Tower.'

Brian never knew any of this because it would have driven him to distraction. He had an enormous job trying to persuade John to receive the medal. John honestly thought it

was hypocritical of him to accept. He hated official cere-
monies of any kind because he felt they were false and
phoney and drugs were his way of getting through the day.

At least John turned up at the Palace. That was more than
he managed at the Ivor Novello Awards at London's Savoy
Hotel. I got a panic call from Brian at the office at 11.00am
on the day of the ceremony. Did I know that John and Paul
were due at the Savoy at 12.30pm for the premier British
song-writing award? Yes, of course I did, it was in the diary.
The only problem was that Brian had insisted he was going
to tell the boys and he had uncharacteristically forgotten.
Could I get them there on time? I said it was impossible but
that wasn't a word Brian understood. The idea of delivering a public snub to the whole of the music and entertainment establishment was simply unthinkable. Just get them
there on time, Alistair. Oh and don't tell them that the panic
is because I forgot. Invent some cover story, please.

In Brian-speak, this translated as 'accept the blame for
the mistake yourself and pretend that you forgot'. John was
out at home in Weybridge so I rang him first as he had
further to travel. At least, he would have had if he'd had the
slightest intention of going anywhere. My explanation
about the last-minute call to the Savoy sounded desperately
lame so I was hardly surprised when the Lennon response
was a brief 'Fuck off,' followed by the line going dead.

That left Paul. The telephone rang in the elegant Asher
household in Wimpole Street for what seemed like an age. I
knew Paul and Jane had been out late the night before and,
as the phone rang and rang, my heart sank further into my
boots. Eventually Jane's charming but very protective
mother answered. I know it sounds hard to believe, but I

don't think Paul and Jane were sleeping together at home at that stage. She couldn't possibly disturb Paul as early as this, whatever the crisis. Could I ring back later? My blood pressure rose by several points but I had no alternative but to wait and ring back later. All the time, I could imagine the guests arriving at the Savoy happy in the knowledge they would soon be seeing the two song-writing Beatles in person.

I left it until midday, and rang back and this time I firmly insisted that Mrs Asher wake Paul – please. She reluctantly agreed and a minute or so later a sleepy and very grumpy Paul came on the phone. I burbled out the story I had been practising for the past hour and there was then a very long pause from the other end of the line. For a horrible moment or two, I was terrified he had gone back to sleep. But then Paul said, 'OK, be round in a cab to pick me up in ten minutes' time.' Thank you, Paul, I thought, and when my taxi arrived at Wimpole Street about 15 minutes later there was Paul to answer the door holding a piece of toast but he was suited and booted and ready to go.

'What's the problem? Do I ever let you down?' said his super-cool expression. But we were still late and by the time the cab struggled through the busy lunchtime traffic it was a quarter to one and the organisers were starting to get very worried indeed. I was so fired up by then I manhandled Paul through the pack of reporters and photographers so he was able to get to his seat on the top table just as lunch was about to start. Phew. But my ordeal wasn't over. Paul insisted that I had to have John's seat and share the glittering company of David Frost, Billy Butlin and others. I know they wondered who on earth I was but by then I didn't care. I'd got one Beatle there on time.

THE BEGINNING OF
THE END
10

As 1966 began, we knew the Beatles were changing. They were older and richer and more confident and they were becoming tired of their boxes. The old days of Brian pushing them into night-after-night live performances were on the way out. But no one knew at that stage that by the summer their reign at the world's greatest live entertainers would be over for good. Brian was concerned that he was losing control and he agreed to allow the Beatles their longest break. They did not give any live performances at all until 1 May. And that concert, a 15-minute set at the *New Musical Express* Annual Poll-Winners All-Star Concert at the Empire Pool, Wembley, was the last concert appearance the Beatles were to make in Britain.

After Wembley, Brian had organised a tour of West Germany, Japan, the Philippines and the United States for the summer and a tour of Britain was promised for the autumn. The Beatles returned to Hamburg, for the first time since their extraordinary fame had blossomed, and found themselves fêted by their original fans. It was great nostalgic fun, but after that it was downhill fast. Hurricane Kit interrupted the flight to Japan and the pilot was forced to divert to Anchorage in Alaska. An illustration of the Beatles' popularity arrived when 400 Alaskan Beatles fans besieged the boys in their temporary hotel rooms. George said, 'There's just nowhere we can go on the planet and not be stared at.'

In Japan, the Beatles flew into massive protests as thousands of demonstrators jammed the streets to insist that pop music should not be played in the sacred Nippon Budokan, which was the venue for five Beatles shows in three days. Eventually, a massive policing operation allowed the concerts to go ahead but the military-style backdrop hardly produced the most memorable performances from the boys.

But the strife in Japan was nothing compared to the chaos that awaited the Beatles in the Philippines. The boys were invited to a reception organised in their honour at the Malacanang Palace by President Marcos and his colourful first lady Imelda. Their children were Beatles fans, it seemed. The only trouble was that we knew almost nothing about this reception.

An official from the palace arrived at the hotel to collect the Beatles. They were all still in bed and Brian firmly refused to wake them. We thought nothing more of it until next day when we woke to screaming headlines about Imelda being stood up and the Beatles insulting the whole of the country with their churlish snub. Brian was horrified and he blamed the promoter for not properly passing on the invitation, but by then it was too late. The damage was done.

We got bomb threats and death threats as the stories of how the presidential party and their 400 guests were kept waiting by the Beatles. The promoter announced he was withholding the payment for the concerts. Then the authorities weighed in and insisted we could not leave the country until the tax on the money we hadn't been paid was forthcoming. Brian taped an apology to be broadcast on Philippine television but mysteriously a burst of static prevented it from being seen. We decided to pay the money and run. But that was not as easy as it sounded. Security became distinctly lacklustre and the Beatles party were jostled and kicked as they left the hotel for the airport. The airport manager got in on the anti-Beatles act by leaving the party to fend for itself against an increasingly angry mob. The escalators stopped and this made it more difficult for the party to carry their baggage upstairs. The boys were pushed and shoved and Brian was knocked over at one point in a frightening ordeal. The boys were booed all the way and even when they got on the plane, the authorities insisted they were not going to be allowed to leave. There was an agonising stand-off for 45 minutes before it was finally allowed to take off for New Delhi via Bangkok.

The Beatles were absolutely furious that they had been exposed to such danger. Brian suffered a sprained ankle but the earache he received from the boys was much more painful. Brian was distraught. Even in India they were besieged by fans and became more and more truculent and homesick. When they arrived back at London Airport on 8 July, George Harrison was asked what was next on the schedule. He said prophetically, 'We have a couple of weeks to recuperate before we go and get beaten up by the Americans.'

There is a very funny thing about showbusiness. Just when you think things cannot get worse, they do. The whole Far Eastern experience upset Brian and it changed his relationship with the boys. Brian was left feeling quite ill and had gone off to Portmeirion in North Wales to convalesce. He had gone up in his Rolls with his chauffeur. Suddenly, the story broke that John Lennon had said the Beatles were more popular than Jesus and all hell was let loose.

The quote had been taken from an *Evening Standard* interview that had been published five months earlier in Britain to absolutely no reaction. But an American teenage magazine called *Datebook* had used the material again under a syndication agreement. Only they had taken John's quotes completely out of context and splashed a trailer on the front page that LENNON SAYS THE BEATLES ARE GREATER THAN JESUS. In fact, what he had actually been saying was, 'Isn't it pathetic that we can pull bigger crowds than Christ can?'

The reaction spread across the United States like a forest fire with the most heated fury occurring down in the southern Bible Belt. Scores of radio stations announced they were banning Beatles records and people started organising bonfires to burn Beatles-related merchandise. A so-called 'holy war' against the Beatles erupted. In Mississippi, an imperial wizard of the dreaded Ku Klux Klan said he believed that the Beatles had been brainwashed by the Communist Party.

I couldn't get Brian on the telephone and the news from America was terrible. The Bible Belt was up in arms, the Ku Klux Klan were involved and the whole thing was a step away from a full diplomatic incident. I couldn't cope with this. It was a week before the Beatles' fourth American tour and I was getting panic phone calls to say that the boys would be lynched if they turned up. Television news bulletins were full of coverage from the Southern states with people hurling records on to huge bonfires and politicians and priests delivering threats of divine retribution. It was Beatlemania in reverse and all the more frightening. Brian finally rang me and I had to arrange to get him back from North Wales to London and over to America as quickly as possible.

I organised a private plane from a little airport called Hawarden. It was a difficult time for flights because it was the summer. TWA were on strike. We were using Pan-Am and the planes were all booked solid and there was a waiting list. We gave Pan-Am a lot of business so I pulled a few strings and we found Brian a first-class seat. Getting him to the plane proved more difficult. His driver got lost in the Welsh mountains and he was terribly late arriving at Heathrow, so I found myself having to persuade the airport authorities to let this little plane land on the main runway right next to the Pan-Am jet. The head of Air Traffic Control had about 100 reasons why this was not possible. I tried to explain this was a matter of life and death and involved the future of the Beatles, and fortunately he was a fan. I could have kissed him when he screwed up his face and said, 'Well, all right then. Just this once.' The pilot was so astonished the landing instructions had to be repeated to him no less than six times. Brian was very apologetic when he arrived but even then there was another panic when he got on the Pan-Am plane and then realised he had forgotten his tablets. He had to take one every three hours on strict instructions from his doctor. They were in his suitcase! So I then had to persuade Pan-Am to let me get Brian's Gucci suitcases out on the tarmac and search frantically through them for his precious pills with a plane-load of impatient people watching me. It was not exactly my greatest moment but I found them and Brian and the much-delayed jet were able to take off.

He went to America to try to save the situation. He offered to cancel the tour but nobody really wanted that. Brian left me at Heathrow saying, 'Look after the boys. Tell them it will be all right. I'll sort it out.' I went back into town and we had a meeting. I have never seen them so scared. There had been loads of death threats before but they had never seemed that serious. All of a sudden, the four of them realised what massive targets they were for any loony with a gun. And America is not exactly short of those. Lennon was absolutely shit-scared. They all were. I remember the way they made it clear they were totally together on this. They didn't blame John at all because he had been completely misinterpreted. At that meeting, they were all for pulling out of the tour. John said, 'Does Brian really want the tour to go ahead with all these nutters promising death and destruction? It's our fucking lives on the line. We don't want to go to America.'

I was scared for Brian because I knew he was a potential target as well. On the morning of their flight to America, they really didn't want to get on that plane. It was a very scary time. It brought home to all of the Beatles how very vulnerable they were. For all the millions of people who adored them, the Beatles knew that there were a sad, mad few who would like nothing more than to blow them away. John took to carrying a gun around for a while which caused a few problems. I think if he had ever needed to use it, he would have been more of a danger to himself than to anyone else.

The Beatles' opening press conference took place up on the twenty-seventh floor of the Astor Towers Hotel in Chicago and should have been the usual jokey affair with the boys wisecracking their way through it in their usual easy-going style. But the Jesus affair had set a new agenda. John was to be made to apologise, but that wasn't easy. There was a lot of pressure on John and he broke down beforehand. He told me afterwards that he realised for the first time then that he wasn't as tough as he thought he was. 'I never wanted to retract a frigging word,' he said. 'It was all true. I was just saying how crazy it was that the Beatles had becoming more popular than Jesus. But then this massive row kicked off and they kept accusing me of blasphemy. To be honest, I never gave a shit what they accused me of but I imagined some religious nutter would take a shot at one of us and that would be all down to me. I didn't want that so I went through with saying sorry.'

In the press conference, John struggled to justify himself but he was on the spot and in the end he had to say the one word which he always found hard to drag out – sorry. But anyone who was at that press conference knew that sorrow was the last thing John Lennon felt about that affair.

John Lennon did not think he had done a damn thing wrong and they just about had to drag the words out of him for once. And if you listen to the apology, it was very half-hearted. John just about got away with it, but if you ever look at that famous footage you can see John Lennon wasn't sorry about anything.

It was not a happy tour. There were stadium invasions and Ku Klux Klan demonstrations that tarnished the Beatles image. And, more frighteningly, on 19 August, there was an anonymous telephone call that said one or all the Beatles would be shot during the two shows that day in Memphis. During the second show, a firecracker was thrown on to the stage and the four Beatles were all scared stiff. They were playing huge venues to make as much money as possible with the least effort and sometimes, even in America, their amazing pulling power sagged a little. Shea Stadium was left with 10,000 unsold tickets when they had easily sold out all 55,000 the year before. *Revolver* had just been released and the new music was more demanding than the earlier songs. Not all the fans liked this musical advance.

The boys themselves were desperately frustrated. John opened up to me about the agonies of touring. 'What is the point of standing there just for people to scream at us. They

Above: The day the Beatles flew out to the USA. I'm the one in the glasses, beside John.

Below: The Beatles play in America in 1964.

Above: The boys making the film *A Hard Day's Night*.

Below: Fans clamour outside the Scala theatre in London, where the film was being shot. A few teenagers were allowed inside to be extras.

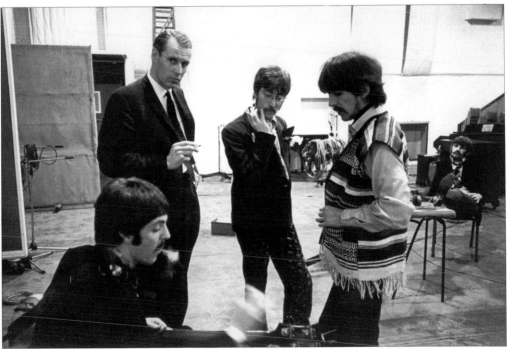

Above: The band, high as kites, with their MBEs. It was a good thing they didn't have to walk the line that day!

Below: In the studio with producer George Martin. George Martin signed the Beatles to EMI after Brian went to see him. Brian was so desperate to get the band signed that he threatened to withdraw his business from EMI if they didn't sign the Beatles.

Above: Taking a break while searching for the magic island in Greece.
Below: Paul's Scottish home in Argyll.

Above: Magic Alexis Mardis, with one of his inventions.

Below: John outside Magic Alex's house in Greece.

A tragic day: Ringo and George attend Brian's memorial service. His death was a shock to us all, especially me, as I was with the doctor when his body was found.

Above: Paul makes his way to Bangor for a lecture by the Maharishi Mahesh Yogi.

Below: John, Yoko and Julian at a rehearsal for the Rolling Stones Rock and Roll Circus. Brian Jones of the Stones watches with them.

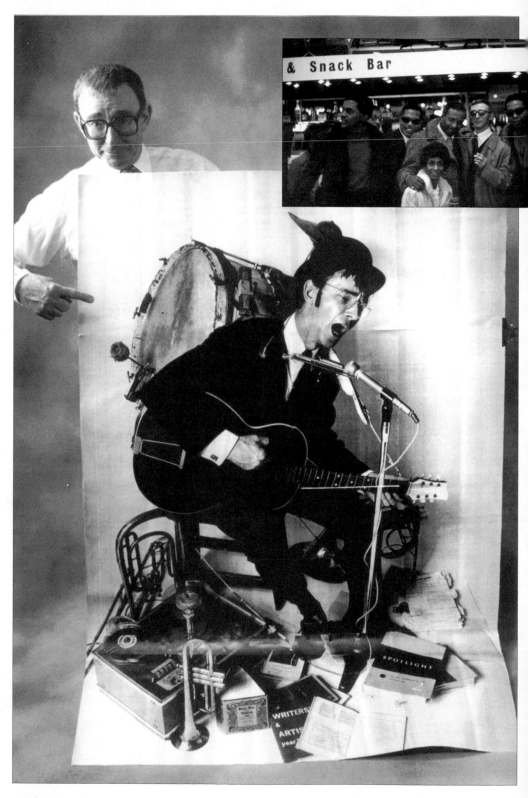

Me today, with the advertisement I posed for, for Apple. The advert was designed to recruit new talent. *Inset*: Myself with the Four Tops.

can't hear us, they can hardly see us. And the whole mad business of hurtling round the world protected by security men and police is driving me out of my mind. I reckon we could send out four waxwork dummies of ourselves and that would satisfy the crowds. Beatles concerts are nothing to do with music any more. They're just bloody tribal rites. What are we doing this for?'

That whole incident was the start for the Beatles of the fear that fame brings. Until then, they had been scared mainly of the prospect of being pulled limb from limb by hysterical teenage girls. That doesn't sound so frightening until you've seen a few thousand of them on the rampage. It is honestly terrifying because the crowd builds up a sort of energy and momentum of its own. Of course, a few young girls are nothing for a grown man to worry about, but there would be streets full of them all whipped up into a frenzy and all desperate for a piece of their favourite Beatle.

'I never thought I'd run away from attractive young women,' said Ringo laconically one day. 'But by the time they actually get near us, they seem to be completely out of their brains. I reckon if we'd used this lot in the war, we'd have overrun Germany in about a fortnight.'

But the more sinister threats from religious groups, lone fanatics or any fired-up fruitcake began to prey on all their minds from then on.

Cynthia was very frightened about what might happen to Julian. She realised he was a prime kidnap target and she installed guards who watched the house very early on. John objected at first because he didn't like anybody watching what time he came in, but even he saw the wisdom of it.

The news footage from the United States after the 'more famous than Christ' publicity was simply chilling. George was always the most reluctant Beatle. He loved the music and he certainly enjoyed the girls on the road, but he hated the intrusion that came with being a Beatle. Several times he quit and each time Brian managed to cajole him back into the group. Brian always told George how much he would be letting the others down, how the Beatles would die if he ever left them, how the wonderful music he was making would be such a great loss to the world if he quit. Brian could be very persuasive when he put his mind to it. But the longer George went on, the harder it became for him to stop. Ringo wasn't too fazed by the fame. He never was the brightest star in the galaxy, but he was scared by the threats. Nutters would phone in to say they were going to leave a bomb for John or Paul. Or they were going to shoot George or Ringo with a long-range rifle.

At first, we just used to laugh in the office about it and have a joke with the boys about keeping their heads down. It never seemed that serious until we saw the Americans burning albums after John's Christ remarks. Then Brian saw the effect it was having on the boys and told us to be more discreet. We never had a policy as such but I always thought laughing down the phone might be enough to put them off. The boys all became paranoid about their personal safety. I would book them on planes under all sorts of names but it was impossible to hide them for very long. Their popularity was so unstoppable that there was a sort of jungle telegraph that seemed to follow them around wherever they went. You couldn't expect the police to keep anything secret. They spent hours signing photographs for coppers' kids and standing being photographed next to a beaming detective and his family.

No one ever announced that the Beatles final concert of the tour at San Francisco's Candlestick Park on 29 August was going to be the last live concert they ever played. It was a chilly night and the Beatles played for just 33 minutes on a stage built over the second base and caged in by a 6ft-high wire fence guarded by 250 police. In case of trouble, an armoured car stood by. But they closed for the only time on that tour with their favourite finale, 'Long Tall Sally'. And just before they started, as he was running on stage, Paul told my friend Tony Barrow, the press relations man, to record the concert. He only had his little tape recorder used for taping interviews and he was surprised to get the request but he dutifully did his best. To most people, it was just another concert, but to the Beatles, after nine harrowing years and more than 1,400 live concert appearances, it was the end of life on the road. As they later flew out of San Francisco, it was George Harrison who became the band's spokesman as he settled back into his first-class seat and said, 'Well, that's it. I'm not a Beatle any more.'

Brian was never quite the same after that tour. It took an awful lot out of him and I'm afraid his dependence on drugs of all descriptions seemed to grow. The money rolled in as before, but Brian's energy and drive took a real dip. He would stay away from the office much more than ever before, for without the great tours to plan and undertake, he found his own personal workload cut down drastically.

It was a sad decline. He had so many prescribed pills and he took all the other drugs as well. I hated to watch him depending on drugs. I think he knew that the Beatles no longer needed him as much as they had needed him before. He never did get very involved in the studio. He trusted the boys and George Martin to do the business there and he was right to do so. But once the touring stopped, he was certainly left with time on his hands and Brian was never very good at relaxation. I think he could see the end of his involvement.

The Beatles were much more interested in advancing their music, and experimenting in the studio. The contrast between that wonderfully fulfilling work and the lunacy of life on the road simply became so great that the decision to stop touring was inevitable. They were producing the most fantastic songs and Paul said to me, 'We could never do any of this on stage. It's just too complex.' They could not produce *A Day in the Life* on stage or a lot of the *Rubber Soul* stuff on stage. And however cynical they all were at one time or another, the truth is that, deep down, the Beatles were an honest band. They did not want to short-change their fans. The new stuff was simply far more interesting to them than standing up and singing 'Love Me Do' for the 5,000th time.

There never was an official leader of the Beatles, but in the early days it was clear that John Lennon was the dominant member of the group. In a very early interview, Paul even commented that John was the leader. He had a presence and a power that gave him the unspoken authority over the group. John was a genius and, to my mind, the unquestioned leader. Paul McCartney was brilliant and possibly the greatest public relations man in the world.

Lulu was desperate to get in touch with Paul. I was horrified when Peter Brown gave her Paul's number in High Park. I went ballistic at Brown. Private phone numbers were guarded like precious jewels, and Lulu only wanted it so she could ask Paul to appear on her television show.

Mick Jagger and John Lennon were great buddies. They loved this rumour that ran around that the Beatles were the White Hats and the Stones were the Black Hats. You wouldn't mind your daughter going out with a Beatle, but you would object strongly if she went out with a Rolling Stone.

Marianne Faithfull became a close friend of the boys. Brian and I met her with Andrew Oldham on *Ready Steady Go*. She was a beautiful young girl with a fantastic figure. We were in the studio's green room after the show and she came up and really set her stall out at Brian. She had a very, very low-cut dress on and she pointed her charming chest at Brian and got as close to him as decency would allow. She was sadly ignorant of Brian's sexual persuasion but he was perfectly polite to her and was quite impressed. 'She seems a very friendly girl,' he said, 'but I'm not sure I am very keen on having her breasts thrust in my face. Do you think she was trying to tell me something?'

The Beatles' involvement with drugs has been massively exaggerated over the years, but they certainly experimented more than most people. It was Paul who first admitted the truth to the Press in a very unscheduled interview which I tried hard to interrupt.

I had been asked round to see Paul at Cavendish Avenue, but when I arrived the security gates were firmly shut and I couldn't raise an answer on the security intercom. But I knew Paul was in because I could hear his voice. I was forced to resort to climbing over the wall. Not very dignified for a smart-suited executive, I know. But, hey, this is the crazy music business. I scrambled down inside the large and elegant gardens and, to my horror, I heard Paul cheerfully confessing to using marijuana because he found it so relaxing. My heart sank into my shiny shoes when I realised the guy he was talking to was a reporter. With as much confidence and authority as I could muster, which was pretty well zero, I tried to interrupt this impromptu press conference which I was convinced was instantly going to burst the bubble of popularity the Beatles had inflated.

'Er, Paul,' I bumbled, 'could I have a word?'

'It's OK, Al. It's cool,' said Paul without removing the easy grin from his face.

'But, I'm not sure that Brian would ...'

'It's OK, Al. Relax. It's time the truth came out.'

I was horrified, because at this time there had been accusations and colourful stories and all the rest of it but none of the Beatles had stood up and admitted that they used illegal drugs. Paul clearly thought the time for this hypocrisy was over and the reporter's notebook was by now twitching nervously in case this scoop was going to be snatched away from him. Paul introduced me to the reporter and told me to relax and carried on telling the world how much the Beatles enjoyed smoking cannabis. It did create a storm but the Beatles weathered it easily and I came to realise the extent of Paul's talent for public relations. He hadn't talked to Brian or the other three before going public. And for all the notice he took of my nervous warnings, I might as well have stayed on the other side of the wall.

Mind you, when it came to odd requests, John gave me the biggest shock. We were at Abbey Road after a recording session and John laid down his guitar, turned to me and said, 'Alistair, I want you to buy me an island.' I thought this was just another example of the customary Lennon banter and responded: 'Fine, John. What'll it be? The Isle of Wight? The Isle of Man? A Caribbean island?'

He said, 'No, man. I'm absolutely serious. I need to have a place entirely of my own. I want an island with a fresh water supply and green grass.' And he handed me a piece of paper with island, fresh water and grass written on it. This was clearly a plan he had devoted several seconds to preparing. 'I want to build a house on it to get some peace and privacy. Somewhere Cyn and I can go to get away. Oh, and it mustn't be more than two hours from London,' said John. This was an interesting challenge, I had to admit. Not since George had asked me to buy him a church had I been handed such a poser. In that case, George had pretty soon gone off the idea of sleeping on the altar so I could forget all about it. But John was as near to serious as he ever managed to be. I contacted the big estate agents and drew a blank, but a couple of days after John's request there was an ad in the *Times* personal column: 'Island for sale off the west coast of Ireland. The Westport Harbour Board will hold a public auction …'

My instant reaction was that this was yet another Lennon wind-up. The sequence of events was a little too coincidental so I rang Cynthia to see if this was an elaborate John joke. She swore John was not messing around this time. He really did want an island and she liked the sound of their own little Emerald Isle. So before you could say 'Top of the morning' to a leprechaun, I was on a flight to Ireland. The island for sale was called Dorinish in Clew Bay off Connaught. I finally arrived by motorboat to find that this particular piece of real estate was in fact two islands joined by a sand and pebble spit of land and measuring around 30 acres. It was fairly flat, with lovely beaches and a fresh-water spring. If you really wanted to get away from it all, Dorinish seemed an excellent place to go. I took photos, noted that the only sign of habitation was the pile of stones, which was all that remained of the old pilot's cottage. I got the snaps developed and took them out to Kenwood, John's house in Weybridge. He took one look and shouted, 'That's it! I've got to have it! Go and buy it for me, Alistair.'

The only snag was that the auction was the very next day. I couldn't get another flight at such short notice so I had to rush to get the boat train from Euston to Holyhead. Brian's brother Clive arranged for his chauffeur to meet me on the platform at Crewe and give me £800 for a deposit. Only the train didn't stop at Crewe. The poor chap found out eventually and drove all the way to Holyhead getting not one but two speeding tickets and gave me the money there.

When I arrived in Westport by mid-morning, I decided to call on the auctioneer Mr Browne, who had his office in the local milliner's shop. In his inner sanctum tucked away behind the drapery and hats, we struck up a quick friend-ship. He was an elderly man and he had lived in London in his youth and wanted to chat about the capital. I was happy to talk and to share an enormous glass of Jameson's with him. Something positive must have clicked in him as he leaned forward and asked me earnestly, 'Do you really want to buy this island?

'Very much,' I said, 'but I'm only a young businessman and my limit is probably less than £2,000.' If I'd said I was buying it for John Lennon, the price would have been £2 million. Mr Browne looked conspiratorially at me and winked. He said,

'There's a syndicate from Manchester who want to put a casino on our island. The reserve price is £1,550. If you want my advice, you'll let my son, Michael, who is the only solicitor here in Westport, do the bidding for you.'

Something about the twinkle in the old man's eye made me do as I was told. When the auction began, Mr Browne sung the barren island's praises as if he was about to auction Manhattan. I began to regret that I had pitched my limit so low as the bidding went steadily up to £1,000 and beyond. Mr Browne's son was hidden behind a large newspaper, taking no part in the bidding. Finally, the price rose to £1,500 and my palms were sweating. I started to wonder if the Brownes had taken me for a mug by promising to handle my bidding. But I should have had more trust in my judgement.

Father Browne spoke up during a brief pause. 'Any further bids?'

From behind the newspaper, young Browne declared, '£1,550.'

'Done,' came the decisive voice of my friend the auctioneer and I was at least briefly the proud owner of my very own island. There was a gasp that rang round the room at this dramatic end to the auction and the men from Manchester started to protest. I went towards Michael to congratulate him, but he had already left. I left as the Manchester men's uproar grew and telephoned John. He was delighted, especially about the price. Even rock millionaires like a bargain.

I reported back to John at Kenwood and he was over the moon with his purchase. He was anxious to go and visit it straight away, but I was dreading this because it meant revealing to the Brownes and others in Westport that I had not been completely straight with them over the purchase.

But after a few weeks, he pushed me into it. He brought John Dunbar from the Indica Gallery and the three of us flew off to Dublin to get a car to drive us across Ireland. The car was late and we had to wait at the airport. John chatted amiably to a few fellow travellers who were delighted to get the chance to meet a Beatle. 'I felt almost normal for a minute or two,' said John. 'They were Manchester United fans. I was just trying to convert them to supporting Liverpool.'

We got into a large Austin Princess and I swear we could have floated across Ireland without using the engine because John Dunbar and John Lennon were smoking dope and popping pills as if they were going out of fashion. I was terrified that the driver would notice the pot fumes but they didn't care. They just giggled all the way across Ireland. Then we hired an old boat and finally John got to see his island. He jumped off the boat, turned towards me, and said, 'Fucking hell, Al. It's fantastic. The pictures don't even do it justice.' He loved it. We walked all over it with John leading the way. He was like a kid in his enthusiasm. Then suddenly he stopped and yelled at us both to do the same. 'Watch out,' yelled John pointing down at something. 'Don't move,' he shouted. I thought from his reactions he had spotted a land mine, at the very least. But it was a gull's egg and he firmly warned us, 'Don't either of you tread on an egg.' Once John had spotted the eggs we all had to tread very carefully indeed. It seems the wild man of rock was desperately keen not to break any birds' eggs.

It was a wonderful trip. The drugs had worn off by then and this was the old John talking. He was funny and friendly and fabulous to be with. He was wearing his old Afghan coat that he loved and he put his arm round my shoulders and said, 'This island is just great, Al. I'm going to give you a corner of it to build your house to get away from it all. That bit down there,' he said pointing to a little peninsula jutting out into the Atlantic. 'That bit is for you and Lesley. Build a holiday cottage and then you can escape like us.'

Nice idea, but we never did of course. After that first trip, the people of Westport were in no doubt as to who the real purchaser of the island was and the second time we went we got quite a reception. John's friend 'Magic' Alex Mardas was involved by this time, with his plan to build John a house on Dorinish and a 'recording studio which floats a foot off the ground so there are no vibrations.'

We flew this time with Gregory's Air Taxis to a new airstrip which had been built three miles from Westport at Castlebar. We took an architect and a solicitor and John, Alex and myself. Only when we got there the pilot had some difficulty finding the new landing site. Fortunately it was a clear day and he eventually spotted it. Finding anyone on the radio to clear us to land was nothing like as easy. The two brothers who operated the strip were both vets and they were otherwise engaged delivering a calf. When we landed, we were greeted by a full civic reception with the mayor and his council all anxious to meet John Lennon.

I almost began to relax with the satisfaction of a job well done. But then John said, 'What I want now is a boat. If I live on an island, I want my own boat so I can come and go as I please.' I spoke to a few shipbrokers and discovered there was a motor torpedo boat for sale in Guernsey. John really liked the idea of starting his own navy. 'I could sail up the Thames and sink the Tower of London,' he told me, and I was despatched to the Channel Islands to take a look at this floating veteran of the Second World War. It had two huge Perkins engines and it was really fast. It had taken me a couple of hours in an old fishing boat to get to Dorinish. This MTB would get there in about five minutes.

My next job was to transport the gypsy caravan that John had in the grounds of Kenwood over to Dorinish, so I had to arrange for a raft to take it across.

A large scare over Ringo came when I managed to lose him completely somewhere in Paris's Orly airport. He and the family were on holiday in Corsica when I got a call from Ringo demanding to come home early. Evidently the locals insisted on talking in a foreign language and the food wasn't nearly as appealing as it is back home in Liverpool, so Ringo and wife Maureen, son Zak, plus Maureen's mother and the nanny, wanted to come home pronto. Could I fix it?

In those days, there wasn't another direct flight to London for almost a week. So I organised Ringo and his group to fly to Paris and I'd meet them there and bring them home in the private jet. The first part worked like a dream but we had a mix-up with the air taxi company and had to make do with a much slower twin-prop plane. When we got to Orly, Ringo's plane had already landed. But there was no sign of my passengers. I organised a search party, divided the place into four sections and we each went off to track down Ringo and family. But he was nowhere to be seen. It was only when I bumped into Maureen in the café that I found the elusive Beatle. She pointed him out to me. The world's most famous rock drummer was sitting forlornly with Zak on his knee surrounded by a small mountain of hand luggage. I hadn't been there to meet him so he'd booked the party on the next flight to London and was sitting patiently waiting. Once I'd explained the circumstances, he did seem pleased to see me. As for not being mobbed, he'd enjoyed every second of his strange anonymity.

Paul is normally as cool as a cucumber but he was hot under the collar when he failed to recognise the world's most famous saxophone player. We were at Abbey Road for another late-night recording session when Paul suddenly decided that what was needed on one particular track was a bank of saxophones. George Martin agreed and Mal was deputed to ring round the musical fixers and call up some insomniac saxophonists. It took about an hour for the first of them to arrive and after that they came quite thick and fast. Paul and I were walking together out of the canteen when a familiar face loomed enquiringly in front of us.

'Are you a sax player?' asked Paul helpfully.

'Well, some people say I am,' smiled the stranger in reply and ambled on down the corridor.

Paul looked puzzled, so as a jazz fanatic I had to explain, 'That was Ronnie Scott.'

'Shit,' said Paul, with feeling. 'You're joking. Oh, no,' and he rushed back after the living legend and the pair proceeded to become close friends. Ronnie thought the incident was hilarious but it made Paul's toes curl with embarrassment.

Paul never did think much of my dress sense. In the fashionable world of the swinging '60s in London, I was always regarded as someone who was rather straight. Paul nicknamed me 'The Man with the Shiny Shoes' to highlight my conservative dress code. And when I had to play a tiny fleeting part in the Beatles massive world-wide *All You Need Is Love* link-up in 1967, he took special precautions.

I had to pick Jane up from Cavendish Avenue on the way to the big event, which was to be beamed to some 400 million people in 25 countries. I knew my plain old business suit would not be the right thing to wear at a psychedelic party like this, so I took a bright orange shirt especially for the occasion. I tried not to look in the mirror when I put it on, hoping that it wouldn't be the most horrible piece of clothing on view to the world. But when I arrived to collect the delectable Jane, she said, 'Paul's left a shirt for you, Alistair.'

I was indignant. 'I'm wearing one. I've even left my tie at home.'

'Oh that is not good enough,' said Jane sweetly. 'He said that he knew you would dress in straight clothes and you wouldn't want to be in psychedelic gear, so he has bought a shirt for you to wear tonight,' and she produced a beautifully-made silk shirt with a trendily multi-coloured pattern and I meekly accepted defeat.

The event in the huge EMI studio at Abbey Road was fabulous. There were so many famous faces in the room I think I was the only person I didn't recognise. I was ordered to put on a sandwich board with 'All You Need Is Love' in Russian written on it and I hope I got the message across. The party afterwards was so good that I really didn't care.

I realise I'm hopelessly biased but I believe that *Sergeant Pepper's Lonely Hearts Club Band* is the greatest record ever made. The Beatles were at their peak and they concentrated every aspect of that amazing ability on making that album the very best. I think that maybe they knew they would never be that tight again. It took them an age to record and I never saw them pour more effort into anything.

Critics hammered them for filling the lyrics with drug symbolism and reckoned the Beatles must have been spaced out the whole time. Well, the Beatles were no strangers to strange substances but the truth is that when they were working at their very hardest, very few drugs were used. The words on the album were a great deal more innocent than a lot of people believe. 'Four thousand holes in Blackburn, Lancashire' is not a testimony to heroin addiction in the north-west. John had just read a newspaper article which said that Blackburn Council had sent out a guy to survey the local roads and he had counted 4,000 holes which needed filling in! So John added the bit about the Albert Hall and put the 4,000 holes into 'Day in the Life'.

And the same goes for the even more famous 'Lucy in the Sky with Diamonds' which so many people were keen to point out were the initials of a widely-used hallucinogenic drug. Well, one of my personal claims to fame is that I was at Kenwood when Julian arrived home from school and I heard first-hand the origin of the famous song title. The lad brought home a picture he had drawn at school, and when John asked him what he had drawn, Julian replied, 'That's my girlfriend Lucy, in the sky.' And John asked him, 'What are all those things around her?'

'Those are diamonds,' said Julian. That's what happened and never for a second did I imagine that such an innocent phrase would ever be the subject of such massive controversy.

The album cover for *Sergeant Pepper* had its own problems when the Beatles decide to feature scores of famous faces. The boys just looned around and drew up a fantastic list of names of people they wanted on the cover. The boys were there themselves, of course, along with wax models of their younger selves from Madame Tussaud's, Marilyn Monroe, Diana Dors, Fred Astaire, Bob Dylan, Marlon Brando and Laurel and Hardy to name but a few. Everyone recognises them. And you might even pick out Shirley Temple, Max Miller and Karl Marx. But would you know the singer Issy Bonn, or Albert Stubbins? Albert was a Liverpool footballer whose main claim to fame was the record transfer fee he cost. And the Beatles couldn't use any of those people's faces until we had found them or the executors of their wills and paid them a halfpenny each for the privilege. You can imagine what a nightmare that was for Wendy Hanson but she tracked them all down in the end.

Brian Epstein was the most charming man I've ever met, but there was definitely another side to him. I encountered the other Brian when he flew into a rage with me at Heathrow Airport on a very sad Sunday morning. Brian had despatched me there at 6.00am to meet two American musicians he had arranged to bring over. Only, when I arrived there was no sign of them. Eventually I heard a call over the tannoy asking for the NEMS representative to go to Immigration. These two jokers had spent all the money Brian had advanced them and turned up without any of the right entry papers. The Immigration official wasn't remotely impressed by my appeal to his better nature, or natural fairness, or the music business. He didn't even want any tickets to a Beatles concert. He wasn't going to budge. These two were about to be sent back out of the country any minute, so I did the only thing I could think of. I rang Brian.

By then it was around mid-morning and Brian arrived, immaculate as usual, even though I'm pretty sure he was still on his way home from his Saturday night out. He took a look at my unshaven scruffy state, sniffed, and told me he would deal with me later. He swept into Immigration and whatever he said to the officials certainly worked. The musicians were in and were sent off to their hotel.

Brian returned to me with steam coming out of both ears. He had that look of tightly controlled anger that I hadn't seen since I had double-booked the Beatles back in 1962. 'Just look at you,' he snorted. 'You're a disgrace to the business, coming to an airport like that. You're not even shaved.'

This time I was so furious at this unjust reprimand I answered back. 'There was nobody here to notice my appearance at six o'clock this morning, Brian. You led me to think it would take five minutes to put them in a taxi so I didn't dress up. Do you realise I have spent five hours trying to get them into the country?'

'I don't care what time it was,' said Brian. 'When you represent me and the Beatles, you dress properly. We must maintain the highest standards at all times. Don't you remember the lecture I gave the Beatles when they signed the contract? The same applies to you. As for this ridiculous business, why can't anybody be trusted to carry out a simple task? Nobody in this country can do anything at all. It's time to set it right.'

I realised Brian was seething at whoever had made a mess of the musicians' visas. He asked me, 'Do you have any sixpences?' I gave him some and he strode over to a row of pay phones. I watched, transfixed as he dialled a number. He just said, 'Good morning. This is Brian speaking. Just to let you know you are fired.' He put the receiver down and went through the same process over and again until he had sacked the entire board of directors of NEMS, with the solitary exception of his brother Clive. I couldn't believe what I was witnessing. He was cutting NEMS to shreds all because of a mix-up over two guitarists who looked like a waste of space anyway.

Then he turned to me and said that I was fired, too. I was furious now. I said, 'Good. Because I don't want to stay to be treated like this. I have been up since the small hours of the morning working for you and if you think you can find someone who can do the job better then that is fine. I've had enough. You can stick your job. I'll be in tomorrow morning to clear my desk.' I started to walk away and I could hear Brian shouting behind me, 'Alistair, come back. Let's talk.' But I was so angry I couldn't have talked and I was on my way out. He rang me a couple of times at home that afternoon trying to make peace but I was still fuming. It wasn't until the next day when I went in to get my things that we talked. I had got the contents of my desk in my briefcase when Brian came into my office very crestfallen. 'Please come back, Alistair. No one can fix things for the Beatles like you.'

Naturally, I gave in on the spot. I always was a sucker for flattery, and I think I understood that Brian was at least partly entitled to blow his top the day before. But I had to ask him what he was going to do with all the directors he had sacked yesterday. I left him going through a list of apologies.

The invention of the Beatles always amazed me. George Martin was terrific here. He used his great musical ability to interpret what they wanted. He would always be careful not to put them down. He said to me once when I asked him how it worked, 'They have a gift. I have to help them give it to the world.' Sometimes they would come up with some pretty strange requests. John once wanted a certain sound and he was finding it impossible to describe. It wasn't a musical noise but he just couldn't quite pin it down. He kept disappearing from the studio and wandering round the offices. At last he came rushing back in shouting, 'I've got it.' He was carrying a short-wave radio that he had found in one of the offices and he wanted the crackling sound the radio made to be fed into the board. George didn't raise so much as an eyebrow. He just arranged for the radio to be recorded. I can't think of many producers who would do that!

Just because most Beatles songs are credited to John and Paul as composers, it is wrong to think that George and Ringo did not contribute. I was amazed sitting silently in the studio that, although John or Paul were usually clearly the driving force Ringo and George were not simply sleeping partners. They certainly would not just sit there and do as they were told. Ringo might make suggestions about the beat and George would chip in about a particular guitar riff. The whole business of recording was a partnership between the four of them and George Martin. And I reckon that George Harrison would be a major composer in his own right if he hadn't landed himself in a group with two of the finest and most prolific song-writers the world has ever seen. I always used to wish George would assert himself more, but he did not tend to push himself forward.

John and Paul never did actually sit down and write together that much. Generally, one would start something off and then get the other one to chip in later when the idea was more fully formed. But when the pressure was on they could certainly churn it out. Once, EMI were really breathing down their necks for another track and were waving the recording contract at us. John just went round to Paul's house in Cavendish Avenue and sat down with Paul to write a single in cold blood, but that was very unusual. The boys always wanted to give the fans value for money. They tried to produce albums with new songs on them, not just singles and their flipsides.

It was a tough job but someone had to do it. It was 1967 and I was searching the Aegean for a get-away-from-it-all island for the Beatles with the Beatles' technical wizard Alexis Mardas. Magic Alex was one of the many extraordinary characters the Beatles attracted in their heyday. He was a particular friend of John's and very nearly as peculiar. But he was good company and he was Greek. We had a great time doing this recce. Eventually, we found a beautiful island of about 80 acres with four superb beaches. So the Beatles could have one each if they wanted. And it even had four smaller islands circled around it.

The Greek island was priced to sell at £90,000 and it looked like just what the Beatles ordered. But this was at a time of currency restrictions so nothing was as easy as it seemed. The Beatles wanted to take a look for themselves and have a holiday into the bargain and I sprang into action to organise it. Alex went off to Greece to prepare his father's house in Athens for us and to hire a large enough yacht to accommodate Paul and Jane, John, Cynthia and Julian, George and Patti, Ringo and Maureen, Big Mal Evans and his wife, Neil Aspinall and me.

On the way I had a huge row with John who was angry that my wife Lesley was not with us. It was as we changed planes in Paris that he realised she was missing from the party and he gave me a real earbashing. John might have had the reputation of the wild man of rock, but he could be surprisingly sensitive at times. He felt it was wrong that Lesley should be left at home and he ordered me to ring and arrange to have her come out and join us. But Lesley hates flying and she doesn't like feeling like a hanger-on. There were always plenty of those. She knew I was working as well as enjoying the sunshine so there was no way I could persuade her to come. I quietly let the matter drop. We arrived to find Alex with a face full of taramasalata announcing that the motor yacht had been caught up and damaged in a fierce storm around Crete and would not be ready for a few days. So some Athens sight-seeing was swiftly arranged. Only someone kindly told the Greek tourist board of our movements and everywhere we went there were hordes of fans.

We all trooped into a music shop and John darted in and went straight past all the gleaming guitars to buy a bouzouki. The shopkeeper couldn't believe that he had the world's most famous group in his shop, or that all they wanted was this humble Greek instrument. Then Ringo went missing. Neil, Mal and I started to panic but he was in the shoe shop next door trying on a pair of sandals and not being recognised by a soul. Ringo had this relaxed way of going round that seemed to escape notice. His face is distinctive enough yet Ringo could wander casually around and people would not bother him at all. If the others tried it they would cause a riot.

The boat was eventually ready and it really was the last word in luxury. But that first night on board, the weather was stifling. I couldn't sleep in my stuffy cabin so I thought I'd stretch out on deck where it would be cooler. I climbed the stairs in the darkness, anxious not to wake anyone up and suddenly fell on to something lumpy and human.

'Who the hell's that? Get off. What are you doing? Christ, it's hot!'

I'd fallen right on top of Paul and Jane.

'Sorry,' I gulped. 'It's me, Alistair. I didn't realise you were up here.' I tried to get up without standing on anything too embarrassing but there was a little squeal from Jane when I steadied myself with a hand. She said, 'Ouch, keep your hands to yourself, Al.'

As I floundered around, Paul's voice said dryly, 'You should have brought Lesley if you wanted a woman to grope in the dark, Al. Find a spare space and go to sleep.'

I realised then that far from being the first person to come up with the brilliant idea of sleeping out under the stars for a bit of cool axir, I was the last. But at least I did have the sense to get myself out of the early morning sun. I copied everyone else, who had hung their towels over the boat's rails to protect them from the sun. Poor old Mal must have missed that trick. He didn't put up his towel and slept on into the morning and got his face fried bright red like a large angry lobster.

It was one of the most enjoyable holidays I've ever had, even if it was supposed to be work. The Beatles and their womenfolk were the most fun people to be around I have ever known. The joking and banter never stopped. The four boys were like four brothers. They might tease and wind up each other something rotten, but they were as tight a group of people as I've ever seen. To be admitted, even briefly, into their company was to experience a constant good time. They laughed and messed around like kids on their first school trip.

We had a crew who looked after us like royalty. On the second day, the captain anchored in a beautiful little bay for us to go swimming. We plunged into the warm sea for a glorious session of splashing around. As we climbed back into the boat, a steward was present to hand us each a fluffy white towel. I found myself lying next to a quick-drying and extremely relaxed John Lennon. He said, 'Do you know, I always remember when I was a kid and I used to go swimming at the baths, afterwards I always came home and had some porridge. I don't know why, but ever since then I always think of porridge when I'm drying off after a swim!'

It was only about 15 minutes later when a beaming steward came out to where we were all sprawling in the sunshine. He was holding a large saucepan and following him was another steward with a tray of bowls and spoons, looking just as pleased with himself. You've guessed it – the stewards were bringing us some steaming hot porridge! Who knows where they had found porridge oats in the middle of the Aegean but they certainly came up with the genuine article. Everyone roared with laughter, especially John, who scoffed his bowlful with relish. Even in the 90° heat it tasted delicious. We even scraped out the pan.

Later, Alex was sent ashore in a motor boat to buy as many pads of paper and coloured pencils as he could find in the little harbour town. Paul decided we would have a doodling competition to find out who could design the most beautiful doodles! Everyone joined in and there was total silence for a while.

After a while, we handed our doodles round for the others to judge and analyse. There were all sorts of strange patterns and curves but I was identified as the odd one out for not drawing circles. My doodles were in straight lines. This became the subject of some detailed debate, and some of it was half-serious. I think they thought this free-range means of expression would open a key to the inner workings of each of our minds or something like that. I think they decided I drew straight lines because I was rather straight. Which I admit I am. I'd like to be a genius like John or a brilliant songwriter like Paul, but I'm not. John asked, 'All of our corners are round and all of yours are sharp. They are all zig-zags and squares. Why do you doodle like that?'

'God knows,' I replied, feeling rather puzzled. John spent a long time carefully studying my pathetic doodles, trying to work out why I was the odd doodler out, but he couldn't come up with anything better than, 'It must have been something in your childhood, Al.' I suppose he's right. It didn't seem that important. But after that, he would every now and then look at me slightly oddly and say creepily, 'Ooooh, sharp corners,' as if I was some sort of closet axe murderer.

The darker workings of the human mind did intrigue John. Months later, when we were back in England, he asked me to bring some papers over and when I got there what he really wanted was for me to join him and Julian in a drawing session. We laid on our stomachs on the floor of the kitchen and my corners were still sharp.

After months of hard work and very long hours, the Greek trip for me became a golden time and my happiest memory came late one moonlit night when John, George, Mal and I sat out on deck watching a glorious Greek moon. The captain was holding the yacht steadily on a course towards the beam of light that the moon threw on to the gently rippled surface of the sea. It seemed as if we were sailing up through the heavens right up to the moon, yet never seeming to come any closer. It was a wonderfully relaxing night as George picked out the notes of the Hare Krishna chorus on his ukulele and John, Mal and I quietly chanted the words. Beatlemania seemed to have finally been left far behind and we were totally at peace with the world as we sat there with legs crossed in the lotus position, staring together up at the shining column of marvellous moonbeams. We must have drifted on like that for a couple of hours until I clumsily broke the silence, 'Just look at that moon.'

John Lennon couldn't resist as he responded laconically, 'Well spotted, Alistair.'

We all fell about laughing and from that day onwards it became my catchphrase. Whatever I pointed out to the boys, the chances were that the response would be a mickey-taking, 'Well spotted, Alistair.'

When we finally arrived at the magical island that was for sale, the boys were instantly under its spell. It only had a fishing village with a few hundred occupants who were friendly and hospitable but mercifully not overly interested in the Beatles. The party was able to wander around drinking in the sublime tranquillity of the place. To visit that island was to fall in love with it and that is what the Beatles and their womenfolk proceeded to do. I was swiftly ordered to get on with the purchase without delay.

But when we got back to London, we discovered that while the Government would allow us to spend the £90,000 they would not sanction the extra expense necessary to build homes and the planned recording studio. We got a letter signed by James Callaghan detailing this great concession in view of the boys' services to exports and the recording industry. I'm sure that Brian could have diverted money that was already held abroad. But Brian was rather straight about things like that and he firmly refused to break even the spirit of the law, let alone the letter. The Beatles battled on for weeks and I was endlessly occupied by the project. We got lawyers' opinions, drafted appeals, and tried to recruit support for the purchase. Then Neil came to me with the news that the Beatles were fed up with all the aggro associated with the island and wanted to forget the whole thing.

Brian opened a private office devoted entirely to the Beatles in a place called Hille House, just off Albermarle Street, and I moved my base there. It was much more peaceful, particularly because the fans didn't know about it initially. I worked there for quite a while with Wendy Hanson and our most frequent visitors were the Beatles themselves. My favourite guest was young Julian who would call in with John, or Cynthia. He was a boisterous little lad and he used to enjoy starting his visits by crashing me to the ground in a rugby tackle. We had a happy little routine whenever he arrived that I would get a buzz on the intercom from Wendy if Julian was approaching so I could go out into the corridor to be knocked to the ground. I always had to crash to the ground simulating great agony, which seemed to delight the little lad. If I happened to be inconveniently on the phone then Wendy had to keep him talking until I come out and fulfilled my dream role – punchbag to the Beatles.

The Beatles took up most of my time as far and away Brian's biggest act, but I also helped out from time to time with his other great Liverpool chart-topper, Cilla Black. When I first met Cilla, she was about 21. Bobby Willis was her road manager in those days. They were going out together but this was long before they got married and sometimes it seemed it was a very stormy sort of romance. On three separate occasions, I had to rush over and act as peacemaker after they'd had another bust up. Each time when I arrived at the theatre, they were sitting on opposite sides of the room, firmly refusing to speak to each other. I'd have to talk to Cilla first to find out what had gone wrong from her point of view. Then I'd cross to Bobby and get his version of events. I'm not a therapist, but just by talking I seemed to be able to get Cilla and Bobby back together again. They were potty about each other even then, but they both had a great knack of letting rows escalate. Usually, I'd do a bit of chatting and then I would announce, 'Right. We're having lunch, now.' And the three of us would sit down to a meal. And that was it. So I always used to claim that I had saved their marriage even before their wedding day. They just needed someone to bang their heads together and Brian decided that was another job for Mr Fixit.

Brian really worked his artists hard. Cilla was doing a summer season at Blackpool which was a big booking. She was second top to The Bachelors from Monday to Saturday and, on Sunday, Brian had booked two concerts in Great Yarmouth, backed by Sounds Incorporated, another of our groups.

I was in London when I received a tearful telephone call from Cilla. She was very upset and told me, 'Bobby has gone to Liverpool.' She was in floods of tears because they had had a huge row this time and he had told her it was all over and had driven back home. I discovered that this time the trouble was serious. Bobby was convinced Cilla had been flirting with Adam Faith, who was also appearing on the bill in Blackpool. Things became more fraught by the second.

Naturally, I was anxious to be as helpful as possible to one of Brian's favoured stars, but definitely didn't want to become involved in a potentially disastrous domestic dispute.

'I don't want to go to Great Yarmouth on my own with a driver I don't know,' said Cilla. My heart sank, because I knew her schedule meant being picked up at the stage door in Blackpool and chauffeured through the night to Yarmouth in one of our faithful old Austin Princess limos. I tried to placate Cilla but even as a young woman she was not someone to be easily pacified. She didn't know that the chauffeur wasn't a potential rapist and there was no way she was travelling across the country through the night with someone she did not know. Through the lines of our conversation, it dawned on me that Cilla was really saying that, under the circumstances, she was in serious need of some tender loving care from the management. In case I was in any doubt about the situation, she explained simply, 'I'm not going unless you come up here and travel across to Yarmouth with me.'

I argued for a while but I was already looking at my watch. It was Saturday afternoon and I knew I could just get up to Blackpool in time for the end of the show. I agreed. I got the train and then a taxi and arrived at the ABC Cinema in Blackpool about ten minutes before the show ended. I was met by a very sad and subdued Cilla.

'Has he really gone for good?' I asked tactfully.

'Yeah,' she said. 'And it's about time.'

We climbed together into the large rear seat of the gleaming limo and Cilla perked up a little. She said, 'I'll tell you what, Al. I'd love some fish and chips.'

I agreed we'd stop at the next one and asked the driver to pull over. We stopped and there were crowds of people outside on a busy Saturday night in Blackpool. 'Stay there,' I advised Cilla, like the last of the big spenders, 'I'll get these.' And I stepped out of the car and strode towards the fish and chip shop. I was just walking across to the front of the shop when this raucous Liverpool voice rang out after me, 'Hey, Al. Will you get us a bottle of lemonade an' all.' So much for keeping the star's identity under wraps.

We sat in the back of the car eating our chips and sharing the lemonade and it was one of those magic nights. Cilla was fresh and funny and had all the charm that has since turned her into one of Britain's favourite stars. And although her marriage to Bobby Willis was to become one of the happiest in showbiz until his tragically early death, I have to say that that night she did not seem deeply disheartened by his sudden disappearance. Eventually she dozed off gently with her head on my shoulder and every time I saw her afterwards she would joke about the night we slept together from one side of the country to the other.

The following day in Great Yarmouth, I was prevented from taking Cilla to lunch at the Carlton Hotel by a pompous head waiter who insisted I wear a tie. I was irritated partly because I was wearing a very expensive turtleneck sweater. He wanted me to wrap a tie around the neck of my sweater. Cilla said, 'You're joking. Don't be so silly. He's one of my managers.' But the guy wouldn't budge.

I never did find out if Cilla really had been flirting with Adam Faith. When I gently raised the subject, she gave me a wink and there was a distinct twinkle in her eye. But she and Bobby were back together again by the following week, and he even thanked me for taking such good care of her.

Cilla became really so fed up with Brian because she felt he was concentrating all his efforts on the Beatles. She accused him of tunnel vision. Gerry threatened the same thing but Cilla took it further and said she was tearing up the agreement. So Brian took drastic action to keep Cilla – he bought her a colour television set and took her and husband Bobby out to dinner.

If Brian had lived, then the whole Apple débâcle would never have happened the way it did. The plans to set up Apple began when Brian was still alive, but he wasn't involved. He didn't want to know about Apple. This was the boys' own project. But if he had lived, he would have stepped in and explained to them that they were going crazy. With Apple they were rudderless. But they wouldn't listen to Neil, or to me. If I objected to anything particularly crazy, they would just say to me, 'Oh don't be a drag, Al.' In the next breath, they would bring me back in to do something for them; Brian would have given them the control they needed.

THE NIGHTMARE
11

Brian twice rang me and said he had had enough of life and was going to commit suicide. Both occasions happened on a Sunday. Each time he said, 'Oh, Alistair, I've had enough now. I am just ringing to say goodbye.' I would try to talk some sense into him but the telephone would go dead. I'd dash out and grab a cab and rush round there. He had this marvellous woman called Vivienne Moynihan who was his secretary. Once when I turned up, she was arriving at the same time. I was getting out of one cab and she was getting out of another. Brian had obviously telephoned both of us with the same doom-laden message. We dashed up the steps together and he was just sitting there.

'What are you two doing here on a Sunday?' he asked.

'Brian, you rang us,' I said. 'You said you'd had enough. You were saying goodbye.'

'Oh, don't be stupid,' said Brian indignantly. 'I was just a bit down. Leave me alone.'

I imagine he had decided he would kill himself in a fit of drug-induced irritation and then the drugs had worn off and he had forgotten all about the idea, let alone the fact that he had called me and frightened me half to death.

So when I got the call on 27 August 1967, I had just walked through the door having had an unscheduled extra weekend in San Francisco. I said to Lesley, 'Oh, it's probably just another of Brian's games. But I'd better check.'

I had spoken to Brian 48 hours earlier and he was full of beans about my bringing the Four Tops back to Britain again. He had seemed on top of the world but when I got this phone call I got a funny feeling in the back of my neck that told me I just had to go. I was tired from the flight and I hadn't seen Lesley for a week. At first I thought, Let somebody else go and check Brian's place out. But I had this strange feeling that this one I had to go to and, of course, I was right.

It was the middle of a Bank Holiday weekend. I had just flown back from California when the news came through that something was wrong. I was still dressed in the denim shirt, jeans and sandals I had travelled in when I got a call from Brian's house in Belgravia. I was just giving Lesley a couple of small presents from Los Angeles. I was looking forward to a good long soak in the bath when Joanne New-field, Brian's secretary, rang to say she'd had a call from Brian's house that something was wrong. Joanne sounded shaky as she told me that Antonio and Maria, Brian's butler and housekeeper, couldn't get Brian to respond to knocks on his bedroom door. His door was locked and they hadn't seen him since Friday night. They phoned Joanne because they didn't know what to do. She was heading over there to see if something was wrong.

Joanne said, 'I don't really fancy going. I'm sure he is all right. They swear he is there in the bedroom, though. Will you join me at Chapel Street, please, Alistair? I know you've just come in from the States, but I'm a bit worried.'

I didn't really have a choice and I had a horrible sinking feeling in the pit of my stomach. 'Yeah, of course,' I said. 'I'll have to take a cab, but I'll be there as soon as I can.'

Lesley was pretty unhappy about this. She was used to panic calls from the office at crazy times, but when I'd just walked in after a transatlantic flight and a week away from home, it was becoming ridiculous. She did her nut. I was running after Brian when I should have been looking after her. I tried to be reasonable.

'It will be one of two things – either Brian will have gone out without them noticing or he will be sitting up in bed asking what all the fuss is about. I'll either be a long time or I'll be back for lunch.'

Lesley was convinced that this was Brian just playing games again.

Still, I had to treat the call as deadly serious and I rushed out to grab a cab. Eventually, I managed to get a taxi and I arrived at Brian's house. Joanne opened the door, looking like death warmed up herself, and said just one word: 'Upstairs.'

Now I was worried. I ran up the stairs two at a time and as I was half-way up I heard the sound of splintering wood. Joanne had telephoned the doctor when she'd hammered on the door of Brian's room but hadn't been able to get any reply. The doctor had put his shoulder to the door and forced it open in a sensible piece of direct action. I followed him into the room. I saw Brian lying in the bed and the doctor leaned over him. My heart was in my mouth. All sorts of thoughts flashed through my mind. Brian slept on a huge double bed that was really two single beds pushed together to make a huge sleeping area. Brian was lying on his side on the bed. He looked as though he was asleep but I knew straight away that he was dead. A wave of almost indescribable pain swept over me. I've never experienced anything like it before or since. Brian Epstein had changed my life in so many ways. He had changed me from a humble shop assistant into part of the management team of the greatest entertainers of the twentieth century.

The doctor finished his brief examination and said, 'Yes, I'm afraid he's dead.' The pain passed and I felt a terrible numbness come over me. All my movements seemed terribly deliberate and almost slow-motion.

I looked around the room and I saw on the bedside table there were about eight different bottles of pills. They all had chemists' labels. At that time, Brian was taking all sorts of medication. He lived on pills – pills to wake him up, pills to send him to sleep, pills to keep him lively, pills to quieten him down, pills to cure his indigestion. All the bottles had their caps properly in place and all of them were still quite full of pills. There was no empty bottle that I could see. By the side of the bed there was a pile of correspondence that he had obviously been going through. There was a plate with three chocolate digestive biscuits on it and down by the side of the bed there was a glass and a half-full bottle of bitter lemon. There was no sign of a note or a message, no blood, no disturbance of the bedclothes. Brian just seemed to be asleep with the bedclothes over him. He was 32.

The doctor and I searched the room for any evidence of what might have happened to Brian. I found an enormous joint in a drawer and I quietly put it into my trouser pocket. We went downstairs and the doctor called the coroner's office and I told Joanne.

'Oh my God,' she said. 'We've got to get hold of Clive.'

We both knew this was a terrible blow for the Epstein family. Brian's father Harry had died about six weeks before. He and Brian were always very close and Brian and his brother Clive had been heartbroken. I remember, even then, the thought going through my mind was that Brian could not possibly have taken his own life. He could never have done that to his beloved mother Queenie. She had been devastated by the loss of her husband and had just been down to London to stay with Brian. The whole family had been devastated by Harry's death. Brian could never have intentionally brought more grief on his mother so soon.

I poured myself a large brandy and tried to think things through. Suddenly, I realised we must have the news broken to Queenie as gently as possible before the whole thing reached the news media. It became the most important thing in my life to let Clive and the family know what had happened before some half-baked news bulletin or pushy reporter arrived to smash Queenie's life to bits. The Beatles were all in Bangor, north Wales, with the Maharishi at his transcendental meditation conference. They had to be contacted, of course, but it became more important to first get the news through to Queenie. Brian was her favourite son, and she was still reeling from the death of Harry.

We rang Clive and there was no reply. I rang Brian's house at Kingsley Hill, hoping to catch either Peter Browne or Geoffrey Ellis, two of the senior figures in NEMS Enterprises, but they were out, too. It was a terrible position to be in. And then, suddenly, it got worse.

The doorbell rang, I opened the door and there stood a reporter. 'Hello,' I said as calmly as I could manage, while inwardly cursing whichever miserable paid informant had sent this unwanted visitor round at such a terrible time. 'I hear Brian's ill,' said the reporter cheerfully.

'Not at all,' I replied with as much confidence as I could muster.

'What are you doing here on a Sunday morning, then?' he responded with more directness than charm.

'Oh, he called me over to go over some papers,' I heard my voice saying. 'But he's gone out for a drive.' I was determined to keep Brian's death quiet just long enough for the news to be broken gently to Queenie. As I said it, I prayed that the doors of the garage were shut and that no one would think to look in to see if Brian's Bentley was there.

'All right,' he said, with a disbelieving look, and off he went, no doubt to try to find a way of checking my flimsy story. I rang Lesley and she completely broke down when she heard the news. She had great respect and affection for Brian even though he had a habit of disrupting our lives.

'I'm going to be a long time,' I told her.

About half-an hour-later, a messenger arrived with a parcel containing my dark suit, white shirt and tie and a pair of black shoes and socks. Lesley had realised that I was still wearing the denims and sandals I'd flown back in from Los Angeles. Bless her.

Still the only people who knew about Brian's death were myself, the doctor, John Galway, Joanne, the police, and the people at the coroner's office. Joanne had whisked Antonio and Maria out of the Press's way in anticipation of the storm which was about to erupt. More reporters were tipped off by goodness knows who that something was very wrong at Chapel Street and they arrived to ask the same questions. By then my explanation that Brian had simply gone out for a drive was beginning to sound a bit thin. Even worse, members of the public heard the jungle drums and a crowd began to gather outside. I remember a young woman with a baby in a pram, just standing looking across the road at the house. There was still no answer at Clive's home and my fears that a reporter would bang on Queenie's door grew by the minute. I just kept dialling Clive's number over and over again. At last he answered.

'Hello, Clive, it's Alistair …'

'Alistair! How was San Francisco? Did you have a wonderful time? Have you seen the Four Tops?'

I cut in as quickly as I could. I'd had an age to rehearse how I would deliver the dreadful news but the words still came out as a burble.

'Clive, there has been an accident.'

'Oh, what? Not Brian?'

'Yes, it's Brian.'

'Is he all right?'

'Clive, he's dead.' It sounded terrible but what else could I say?

Clive let out a long and terrible scream and dropped the phone. Barbara, his wife, picked it up. 'Alistair, what on earth's wrong?'

I told her and asked her to contact Queenie before the reporters did.

'Don't you worry about us,' she said and put the phone down.

By the afternoon, the news broke and my little charade was forgotten. At least I had bought enough time for Brian's elderly mother to hear about the tragedy in as kind a way as possible. The crowds of Press and public outside the house now numbered thousands of people. Reporters were clamouring for a story and nothing I could say sounded right. It was only then I truly realised how close I had become to Brian. I loved him as much as any man can love another without a homosexual link. He had lit up my whole life from the moment I had walked into his office for an interview in Whitechapel, in Liverpool, all those years before. He could be maddening and unfair but mostly he was just a great positive presence who had the drive and the vision to change the world of pop music.

There was a hideous moment when the hearse arrived with a black coffin to take Brian away to the mortuary. The coffin seemed so functional and impersonal, lined with black baize, a mere vessel for the transport of the dead. I had to supervise Brian's last journey from Chapel Street.

At long last I left it to the Press office people to deal with the reporters. By now they were interviewing everyone they could find and the photographers were flashing away at the house. I went home to Lesley and we spent the night remembering all the good times Brian had given us.

'The thing I'll miss is his parties,' said Lesley. 'Everything was always just right. Always.'

The one comical moment in a black day in my life came after I'd been asleep that night for about an hour. Lesley was tidying up and putting some washing in before coming to bed and she suddenly burst into our bedroom screaming my name. I woke up and struggled to gather my senses. I wondered what other nightmares could happen now and then I realised Lesley was holding the huge joint which I had smuggled out of Brian's room. 'You promised me faithfully that you would never ever take any drugs,' she shouted, waving the offending article. 'How could you?'

I don't know if it was the pressures of the day or the hilarity of the moment but I burst into an uncontrollable fit of laughter. Lesley looked even more angry as she witnessed my mirth. But eventually my tears of laughter turned into tears of grief as I cried for my lost friend. Lesley became concerned and came over to the bed to say she was annoyed, but not that annoyed. I explained the origin of the joint and then we laughed and cried some more.

The next day, I went back to Chapel Street and there were rows of flowers that people had left. I gathered some of them to take them inside. On the top step somebody had left five red carnations beautifully placed in a row, with a piece of paper torn from a notebook saying simply, 'We loved you, too.' That finished me. I took them indoors, dashed into the bathroom and cried my eyes out like a young child. After a few minutes I felt better and I put the flowers in water and placed them on a table with the note beside them. I sat and thought for a while. My friend and my boss is dead. I knew that no one could replace him, either as a friend or as manager of the Beatles.

The Beatles had all gone to Bangor on the train on the Friday. They were recent converts to the Maharishi Mahesh Yogi. Patti had encouraged first George and then the other Beatles to try transcendental meditation. It was a way of reaching a state of eternal happiness and peace, some kind of nirvana without drugs. The Beatles had tried most other things in their search for an inner tranquillity, which might make superstardom easier to live with. And this brand of instant relief had them hooked at this stage. They had seen him lecture and go into his own trance at the Hilton hotel a few days before. The Maharishi, who was wide awake enough to recognise the publicity potential of recruiting the Beatles as his new disciples had invited the famous four up to his hotel suite for a private audience afterwards. There was such a crush at Euston Station on the Friday of their departure that Cynthia had missed the train. A policeman thought she was just another crazed fan and stopped her getting on. But with Mick Jagger and Marianne Faithfull in tow as well, the train was followed by TV newsmen and newspaper reporters and photographers. They dubbed the train 'The Mystical Express' as the whole thing began to turn into a circus.

It was Jane Asher who answered the call. The boys had to be told about Brian's death as soon as possible and Jane rushed to get Paul to come to the phone. He seemed shocked but strangely sedate as were the other Beatles. In their surreal setting they seemed to be turning for advice on how to react from the Maharishi who was again swift to make capital. He told them Brian's passing was a good thing and was not to be mourned. He brought them up to date on his views about the material world being in permanent conflict with the spiritual world and then made them crush a flower to demonstrate that all good things could be destroyed. Marianne Faithfull said she felt that the Maharishi instantly exploited Brian's death. She said, 'The Beatles were shattered. I can hardly bear to remember it. I think he actually said, "Brian Epstein is dead. He was taking care of you. He was like your father. I will be your father now." ' These poor bastards just didn't know. It was the most terrible thing.'

George told the reporters who were congratulating themselves on falling over the showbiz story of the year that 'There is no such thing as death, only in the physical sense. We know Brian is OK now. He will return because he was striving for happiness and desired bliss so much.'

Paul was uncharacteristically wooden: 'It is a great shock and I am very upset.'

John said even more coolly, 'Our meditation has given us the confidence to withstand such a shock.' At that time he had been meditating for all of two days. To be fair, John later said, 'I had the feeling that anybody has when somebody close to them dies. There is a sort of little hysterical, sort of hee, hee, I'm glad it's not me or something in it, the funny feeling when somebody close to you dies.' And more prophetically he added, 'I knew we were in trouble when Brian died. I didn't really have any misconceptions about our ability to do anything other than play music and I was scared. I thought, Now we've fucking had it."

The inquest was held on 8 September and I was very relieved when the coroner's verdict was accidental death. He died from the cumulative effect of bromide in a drug he had been using for a long time. The drug was Carbitral. The amount of bromide in him was only enough to be described as a 'low fatal level' but Brian had taken repeated 'incautious self overdoses' which added up enough to kill him. He had been taking more pills than were good to him at that time but I don't believe in a million years he meant to kill himself.

Rumours that Brian had committed suicide started straight away but I've never believed them. He had just had his grieving mum Queenie down to stay with him for ten days and he was very upset by how hard she had been hit by his father's death. Brian was also right in the middle of making plans for her to come and live near to him in London.

I had spoken to him from America several times in the days just before his death. I had gone to the States not for Brian but simply to help Robert Stigwood out. The Robert Stigwood group had just merged with NEMS. Stigwood's group Cream were about to go off on their first American tour. There was a hitch in the paperwork in that they hadn't bothered to apply for proper work visas. I pointed this out and found myself getting the American Embassy to open up on a Sunday to get the correct documents for Eric Clapton, Jack Bruce and Ginger Baker. Stigwood was pushing for me to go with Cream to help smooth the way but I insisted I couldn't go anywhere without Brian's approval. Brian first seemed miffed by the idea and sent me a pompous telegram saying, 'Under no circumstances will you leave for America. Brian Epstein.' I was annoyed because I'd been trying to contact him for a couple of days to ask him directly, but he had been very elusive. Then the phone rang at half-past-two in the morning. It was Brian, over a background of music and laughter. He said, 'Alistair, it's Brian. Wouldn't you just love a week in San Francisco?'

'Brian, I ...'

'I knew you would! Have a wonderful, wonderful time. Call me when you get there. Bye bye!'

Lesley was not amused. I called at the Embassy to collect the visas on the way to the airport. Then there was another surprise. Brian was at the airport. Looking immaculate as usual, he smiled and said, 'Hello, Alistair. Sorry about all that nonsense beforehand. I just thought I'd come and see you off.' And he left in his chauffeur-driven Rolls as quickly as he'd arrived. Brian had come to see me off, and he hated airports even if he was going somewhere. He seemed natural and full of beans which was great, as he had been under the weather for weeks.

There were several conversations on the telephone with Brian while I was away and he always seemed fine. In the last one, he asked me to come home via Los Angeles so I could call in on the Four Tops who were playing the Coconut Grove. He wanted me to ask them to come over and do another tour for us.

Brian never sounded remotely like a man who was considering suicide. Certainly, he had some strange things going on in his private life but I've always felt the rumours about mystery lovers who were there at the end were pure fantasy.

The Beatles met Queenie in Brian's drawing room when they got back from Bangor. They were all very sad and they felt very sorry for her. There was a lot of respect for Queenie. She asked the Beatles not to come to the funeral because she felt the crowds would get out of hand if they did.

The funeral was held in Liverpool and Brian's body travelled up from London by road. It was delayed and there was one comical moment at the service. Cilla, Gerry Marsden and I were among other family members when there was a long and unexplained delay. Time dragged at the sad occasion as the coffin simply did not arrive and Gerry whispered to me behind his hand, 'Trust Brian to be late for his own funeral.' I had a job to suppress my laughter, but it was a respectful joke. Brian always had a reputation of not being terribly punctual and we enjoyed the humour of his memory. But it was the only light moment in a dreadful day.

The debate goes on to this day about whether the Beatles would have left Brian if he had not died. Certainly they did not need him in the same way they needed him before. But I don't believe they would have got together and sacked him. I think there was too much mutual affection, love and respect in there for that. But then, I'm an old romantic.

THE UNHAPPY
ENDING

12

I didn't know what to do after Brian's death. His brother Clive Epstein asked me to stay on as general manager of NEMS Enterprises. It was exactly what I didn't want to do. I was so upset by Brian's death and I knew that the Beatles were never going to be the same without him, so I had decided the best thing for me to do would be to get out and get another job. But Clive and Queenie appealed to me to stay on as general manager until things were sorted out. NEMS was still going. I was one of the longest-serving employees and I was happy to do anything which would help to keep Brian's legacy intact. But this was a desperately unhappy time. Robert Stigwood and Vic Lewis were the two who were likeliest to run things and I didn't want to support either of them. The atmosphere in the office was depressing. There was so much sniping and in-fighting that it was very a unpleasant place to work. The Beatles seemed lost without Brian. He had taken so many of the important decisions for them. And the vultures were already circling the business.

Before he died, Brian had been planning a merger with Robert Stigwood, an up-and-coming pop entrepreneur and manager of the Bee Gees. But they had only had initial talks and Brian hadn't told the Beatles anything at all about any possible link up with Stigwood. There were loads of aggressive businessmen around trying to tell Brian that he should have done better deals for the Beatles. The American Allen Klein made a huge fuss about getting a vastly increased royalty deal for the Rolling Stones.

Brian was not at his old familiar best for a long time before he died. The Beatles' decision to stop touring took away a huge part of his life and he did take his eye off the ball. But Brian never wanted to be the richest guy in the world. His great ambition was to give the Beatles to the world. And he had succeeded in that way beyond even his own vivid imagination.

I felt totally lost without Brian. Some of the other figures seemed motivated by money and they seemed to want to spend their time wheeling and double-dealing. Stigwood asked me very soon after Brian died if I would come to work for him. He seemed to think the Bee Gees were going to go places and he wasn't wrong.

In fact, the first place Maurice Gibb and I went to was a sleazy strip club. He had a very striking convertible, burgundy-coloured Rolls Royce at the time. We had been drinking in DMs, a pub just on the fringes of Soho that was used by a lot of pop people. The car was just parked down the side of the pub, just outside a tatty little strip club. It caught Maurice's eye and he said to me, 'Do you know, Al, I have never been in a strip club.' I used to go to Raymond's Revue Bar in those days and I thought I was a very sophisticated man about town. And I knew what was coming next. Maurice grinned in embarrassment, gestured at this seedy strip joint, and said, 'Should we go in?' We couldn't resist it and we went past the dozing bouncer and into this dim and dank den of iniquity. As strip clubs go it would have struggled to be even third-rate. We got a couple of drinks at the bar and turned to the tiny stage to watch a rather elderly stripper going through her routine. It was about as erotic as a visit to an abattoir and, like a couple of naughty school-boys, I'm afraid we got the giggles. When you really shouldn't be laughing, it's always so much harder to stop and we found ourselves shaking with mirth. We could see that some of the more muscle-bound assistants were not taking too kindly to us laughing at the main attraction so we got to our feet and chortled our way back to Maurice's magnificent motor.

He was a smashing bloke and I would love to have had a role in managing the Bee Gees, but I felt a strong pull of loyalty to NEMS and Clive Epstein. Clive had almost none of Brian's flair or charisma, but he was still a hell of a nice bloke. He wanted me to stay, so I stayed – it was as simple as that.

Eventually, Stigwood met the Beatles and they weren't keen on him taking over control from Brian. They didn't know much about him. They said if he ever managed them, they would just play 'God Save the Queen' until he released them from any contract.

Then, in December, I got a phone call. John Lennon's unmistakable voice came on the line.

'Hello, Alistair. You're looking a bit pissed off at NEMS recently.'

'Yes, John, I am. All the endless in-fighting is really getting to me and nothing is the same without Brian around.'

'Well, why don't you come over and be general manager of Apple,' he said.

My heart leapt. John asked me when I could start and I said, 'Tomorrow.'

Lennon laughed and said, 'When you said you were pissed off, I didn't know you were that pissed off. Welcome aboard, mate.'

We had started to set up Apple before Brian died. In fact, Brian was on the original executive board along with the accountant and the solicitor, Neil Aspinall, the boys and myself. It really started as a way to spend the boys' massive money mountain and somehow to minimise their tax bill. But Brian was never greatly interested by it. They were paying 19s 6d in the pound in income tax at the time and Apple was a way to reduce this to something like 16s. The boys' idea, if that is not too strong a word, was that business should be fun, not just a load of boring guys in boring suits poring over boring figures. They wanted to find exciting, new, original thinkers to give them the platform to develop new products and ideas. Some of the philosophy behind the whole thing was distinctly wacky. Remember, the boys were experimenting with lots of drugs at this time so they weren't always desperately rational. But at heart it was a great idea.

I was delighted to be involved with the Beatles so closely again. And a stylish flat in Montagu Place, just across from Jimi Hendrix's old flat where John and Yoko were later busted, was part of the salary and I was the new general manager of Apple. I prepared myself for a brave new world of building up the Beatles' business without Brian. If only Apple hadn't been such an unmitigated disaster area, it would have been the ultimate dream job.

One of the first big ideas was to set up a chain of card shops selling birthday and Christmas cards and cards for every occasion. In business terms, this has been proved a successful idea many times since, but the boys thought it was just about the most boring concept in the world. I became the link between the boys' brainwaves and the real world and sometimes it seemed to be a huge gap to bridge.

The boys decided they'd have people they liked around them, so I was ordered to find the telephone number for

Derek Taylor, the colourful former Press officer who was now happily installed in California and heavily involved with the Byrds and the Beach Boys. They crowded into my office to make the call like a group of kids organising a party. It was the middle of the night in Los Angeles but the boys didn't care about boring details like that. Once Derek was roused and brought blearily to the telephone, the Beatles took the receiver in turn to sweet-talk Derek into coming back into the fold.

Then Paul persuaded me to undertake a modelling career. It only lasted for one job but it was certainly fun. His idea was for adverts in the *New Musical Express* saying 'This man has talent' with the picture of a very straight, suit-wearing, bowler-hatted businessman who had allegedly just broken into the music business. Paul wanted to encourage even the most conventional of creatures into throwing off the shackles of everyday life and plunging into the unknown with the assistance of this wonderful organisation called Apple. Naturally, the straightest guy Paul knew was 'the man with the shiny shoes' – yours truly. So I was sent out to buy a bowler and Paul rigged me up as a sort of one-man band for his advertising campaign.

The photo-session was hilarious. There I was, strapped into the one-man band kit, with a great heavy drum on my back complete with cymbal, guitar, mouth organ, the lot. I sat precariously perched on a stool with all the clutter any singing accountant might have lying around the house – euphonium, French horn, trumpet, violin bow, manuscript paper, copies of the *Writers' and Artists' Year Book* and *The Stage*, and a cheap recorder all ready to record my music for posterity.

It did occasionally cross my mind that Paul was taking the mickey, but that was nothing new and I didn't really mind. We tried quite a few poses with me sitting there looking creative and feeling like a prune, but Paul said that they were no good.

'It's no good if you're not really singing. Sing us something. Anything you like,' he enthused.

The only time I ever sing is in the bath and I couldn't even think of what to sing. I settled on 'When Irish Eyes Are Smiling' and just belted it out trying not to die of embarrassment. The photographer clicked away happily.

At the end of the session, Paul and I walked out into Soho and I was still flexing my shoulders to try to get the circulation back after having the drum strapped on to me. And I'd forgotten I was still wearing the bowler hat until Paul snatched it off my head, threw it into the middle of the road, and started jumping on it. 'I've always wanted to do that,' he said, and we both fell about.

There are loads of magical memories from my time with the Beatles and that is one of my favourites. It would never have occurred to me to jump on a bowler in the road, but the pleasure it gave Paul makes me smile even today.

When we'd stopped giggling, he took me round to tailor Dougie Millings, the guy who made the Beatles' suits, and told me to choose any cloth I fancied. He then designed a suit for me, told Dougie to take the measurements, to finish it as quickly as possible and charge it to his account. That can't be bad, I thought, a brand-new suit in exchange for a few minutes dressed as a one-man band.

Mind you, when I saw the ad all over the back page of the *New Musical Express* my jaw dropped. Paul had gone into full creative overdrive when he had composed the copy for the advert and had written that I'd had talent and now I was driving a Bentley thanks to my musical genius. I wish.

Apple was a truly bizarre place to work. Alex Mardas was one of the most amazing people. He was definitely way ahead of his time. He designed a telephone you could use without touching. You just spoke the number into it and it rang up whoever you wanted. I know they're around now, but in 1967 this was remarkable stuff. Then he turned polystyrene ceiling tiles into a really effective loudspeaker and even an electric spoon that you could leave stirring while you got on with preparing the rest of the meal. Alex was unbelievable.

But the Beatles were always better at getting rid of money than anything else. George was always a keen car enthusiast and he began the rush to buy a Mercedes. He really wanted a Rolls-Royce but he soon lost interest when the snooty salesman told him there was a 14-month waiting list. George tried Mercedes instead and received an instant lesson in German efficiency. He fell in love at first sight with the huge new Mercedes 600 model. It had power everything – brakes, steering, windows, seats, air-conditioning. It was more expensive than the Rolls and George wanted one in black. There was just a five-day wait while Mercedes specially contoured the driver's seat to fit George's back. It was delivered to Kinfauns, his fabulous home near Esher, within a week.

Like anyone with a new car, George wanted to show it off. He rang Ringo who was mightily impressed. Within another six days, he had one, too. Then John saw the two cars parked together and he decided it was time he joined the club. I don't think Mercedes could believe their luck.

Paul decided to buck the trend and stuck with his Aston Martin DB6 and his sweet little custom-built Mini. It was the only Mini I ever knew with its own record player!

The Beatles all loved to buy, buy, buy. With George it was houses that were always taking his fancy. He alerted me one day that we were going to look at a mansion in Kent. I said, 'You can't go in person first time, George. The price will go through the roof. Or the locals will organise a petition to keep you out.'

'We won't be recognised. Pick you up at ten tomorrow. Just organise the appointment, please, Alistair.' And the phone went dead.

The following morning, just as I was waiting for George, I was irritated to get the message. A young woman was asking for me in reception. I went down to quickly get rid of whoever it was. Standing in the lobby with her back to me was a young woman in a very expensive but somewhat severe twin-set topped off by a pillbox hat. She looked the very epitome of respectability and squareness – until she turned towards me and I saw it was Patti Harrison, dressed evidently for an investiture. 'Meet your wife for the day, Alistair,' she smiled. 'Now come and meet James, the chauffeur.'

Outside the front door, standing conspicuously on the double yellow lines was the enormous Mercedes 600 limousine which George had recently bought. At the wheel, staring dutifully straight ahead was our liveried chauffeur complete with peaked cap. Patti opened the door and I held it while she climbed in. He's not much of a chauffeur, I thought. Aren't they supposed to hold the doors open for us? Then the driver turned round and I was confronted by

George's beaming face. 'Where to, wack?' he said. Not a trace of the famous Beatles hair was to be seen. It must have taken him hours to pin it under his cap.

We swept off to a very expensive section of the Kent countryside where it turned out a magnificent pile owned by a stockbroker was for sale. His very county wife sprang to show newlywed Mr and Mr Alistair Taylor round the property and the chauffeur stayed at the wheel.

Patti and I tried to behave like a happy couple and talked enthusiastically about what we would like to do to the house. But we had some awkward moments. As we toured the expansive garden and approached the tennis court the houseowner said, 'Do you play tennis?'

Patti said, 'No.' I said, 'Yes,' but I supposed she would understand that we don't have to do everything together. In the end, it was a lovely house and I thought we got away with our little charade rather well. Right up until the moment we were leaving when the house's elegant occupant said, 'Are you sure Mr Harrison wouldn't like to see the house as well.'

The Beatles were never boring to be with but sometimes they were pretty dangerous. One of John Lennon's personal crusades was to persuade me to turn on, tune in and drop out to acid.

There was a little pub round the corner from the early Apple offices. Before we moved to Savile Row, our first offices were temporary ones in Wigmore Street. At that time John used to come round and would want to go for lunch. He had just discovered the mind-expanding excitement of acid. And with the enthusiasm of the recent convert, he wanted to show me how fantastic it was. John knew I was straight. I had never smoked a joint. I had never taken acid. In the pub, the onslaught started. John and Derek Taylor had decided it would be a good idea if I went on an acid trip. They kept saying, 'Al, it's mind-blowing. It's incredible. You've never experienced anything like this in your life before.'

I said I did not want to know. Call me a coward if you like, but I didn't think a doped-up popstar was going to be the most reliable minder if anything went wrong inside my brain. If I decided I could fly from the top of a high building, I'm sure John would have been the one urging me to take off. I'd heard about people pretending they can fly. I never touched pot or speed. He and Derek spent weeks trying to get me to go on an acid trip. John kept saying, 'Come on, Al. We'll be with you. We'll look after you.' Finally, they gave up.

We had some very snobby neighbours in Savile Row and the boys used to love to wind them up. Whenever we had a new piece of music to listen to, which was pretty often given our business, they always made sure the windows were wide open and the volume was turned right up. We would get telephone calls from our frightfully upper-crust neighbours demanding, 'I say, could you turn that awful racket down,' and the Beatles would roar with laughter.

We had enjoyed such a good working relationship with the police that one of the few times I rebelled against the lads was during a rooftop concert when they insisted on secretly filming the boys in blue. I thought that was wrong and I still do. The boys loved defying authority. It was a natural inborn instinct to stand up for yourself. They were forever being told what they had to do, and standing up and saying, 'Fuck off. We don't have to do anything you say. It's our lives to do what we want with.' But generally they would go along with it. They decided not to film overtly but covertly instead. They put a booth in reception to secretly film the police's reaction and I didn't like this. I tried to protest that in spite of what they might think about coppers, we owed them a lot for their help over the past years. But they wouldn't listen to me, as usual. This was just before the rooftop concert and I watched that from the post-box on the corner. I didn't want to be part of any plan to take the mickey out of the police. I thought it was wrong.

Magical Mystery Tour might not have gone down in pop music history as one of the Beatles' great successes but it was one of the happiest episodes. Paul rang me one day and asked me to come round to Cavendish Avenue. He said, 'I've had this idea. Do they still do mystery tours on buses.'

I had no idea but I was prepared to find out. Paul had this happy memory from somewhere of getting on a coach and paying five bob and being taken off who knows where. At Paul's request, I took Lesley down to the seaside for a week to investigate whether they still existed. Paul's idea for MMT was to have a coach trip complete with courier saying, 'If you look out to your left you will see such and such a castle and so on.' Paul thought this would be a great starting point for something magical then to happen. 'And we will be the four magicians creating all this.'

I thought it was a fantastic idea, I genuinely loved it. So Lesley and I went off to Eastbourne. I loved the place and always used it as my bolt-hole. If ever life got a bit too hectic, Lesley and I would go off for a few days to the

Queen's Hotel in Eastbourne and it was the one place I never gave Brian the number.

This time it was a Sunday and, just our luck, the rain was bucketing down. I happened to glance out of the window at a fairly empty car park and in pulled this gaudily coloured bus. It was bright and packed with people and it looked elderly with a sort of faded style, just as Paul had described to me. It was citrus yellow and hideous blue. I just dropped my knife and fork and shouted, 'I've found it.' Lesley knew what I meant and sighed as I went running out into the pouring rain and jumped straight on the bus. 'Do you hire this bus out?' I blurted to the astonished driver. 'Yes,' he said as if he was speaking to someone so stupid he didn't know what function buses had in the scheme of things. I was so excited I ignored the sarcasm and got a card with the operator's name, address and telephone number. The coach was owned by a firm called Fox's of Hayes.

The following day, I rushed back to London with the good news for Paul and we hired the bus. At that stage, this was just one of those mad McCartney schemes. He hadn't even told the other boys what he was planning.

This was the period when the Beatles spent a great deal of time stoned on acid so there wasn't that much sensible communication going on. But Paul won over the others. His idea was that we would have genuine old-age pensioners and underprivileged children on board. Paul had also recruited Ivor Cutler and Nat Jackley. And I had been meeting and auditioning people, such as an accordionist. The idea was for Paul and the others simply to slope off with a skeleton camera crew and record the action as it happened. Hotel stops were booked. Then the others all started throwing ideas in and the whole thing got out of hand. If you watch it at the beginning, our bus from Fox's of Hayes has all these psychedelic coloured panels stuck on it but towards the end some of them had disappeared. This was because they blew off as we were hurtling round the countryside.

One night they were down in Newquay and I got a phone call from Neil Aspinall. They desperately needed a Mae West life-jacket for a sketch to be recorded tomorrow. I was in the West End and they were right on the coast, yet it became my job to find this particular piece of nautical equipment. That was one of the penalties of being Mr Fixit. I legged it round to Albemarle Street where I knew there was a sailing shop. But then I had the problem of how to get down to Newquay. I called the chauffeur and decided to take this life-jacket down in person. It's a long journey, even in the back of a limousine. But when I arrived I marched proudly into the lounge of the hotel pleased with myself for delivering this vital costume only to be told by John, 'No, Al. We don't want the old Mae West any more. We've gone off that idea. But it's great to see you. Have a drink.'

That was fairly typical Beatle behaviour. One minute something would be required instantly and it was incredibly important that it was provided. The next minute, they would lose interest and be panicking about something completely different. 'Take it back with you tomorrow,' laughed John.

A lot of it was filmed at West Morley airbase. The final scene, with 'Your Mother Should Know', had the Beatles resplendent in wonderful white suits and top hats and tails with a whole mass of people in this hangar going up a big white staircase. The boys kept their outfits a secret because they wanted to surprise everyone and they certainly did that. It was breathtaking. Paul was mad about Busby Berkeley at the time so we had the whole of the Peggy Spencer Formation Dancing Team. We invited all the people from miles around and thousands came. The idea was that the four boys appeared for one last time in the Magical Mystery Tour bus with a great crowd following them like the Pied Piper of Hamlin. There were grannies and women with babes in arms and gangs of Teddy boys, all sorts had arrived. We were just setting up this big finale when suddenly there was a power cut and every light in the place went out. It was Sunday afternoon. We needed another generator and we got one just in time, just as the crowd were losing interest and starting to drift away. We were just ready when suddenly every light went out again. More people left and by the end there were about 25 of us trying to make ourselves look like the sort of crowd you usually see at Wembley. If you look very carefully you can see me, Cynthia, little Julian, Big Mal, Neil and a few others desperately trying to make ourselves look like a crowd.

It was a fun time filming *Magical Mystery Tour*. Paul wanted another scene in a strip club with the Bonzo Dog Doo Dah Band, so I persuaded Paul Raymond to let us use his Review Bar early in the morning. We had a young lady ready to perform and things were just getting going when two gentlemen from the technicians' union arrived to stop us filming without union permission. They said we should have a crew of 32 and we only had about three guys. They were very unhappy. 'We will black this and it will never be shown if you carry on without the proper manning levels,' he said. The union sent the cost spiralling by thousands of pounds as we had to pay all these people we did not want and did not use. Paul was very angry.

It was so much fun but the BBC showed it in black-and-white which was very strange because the whole point of the thing was the colour. I just don't know why they haven't shown it again. Afterwards, I was instructed by the boys to organise a party for everyone who had anything to do with it. That turned out to be quite a do. It was at the Royal Lancaster Hotel in Bayswater Road and, as it was heading towards Christmas, they decided to turn it into the Christmas party for all the Apple employees. That meant more work. Then John rang.

'Al,' he said. 'We're making it fancy dress.'

Great, I thought. I hope that's the end of the instructions. The invitation list seemed to get longer and longer. Freddie Lennon arrived, and was pissed out of his head before very long. He went up on the stage and fell flat on his face, which just about brought the house down.

I sat on Paul's table with Jane and her parents. A couple of weeks later, Paul rushed into the office having seen a 'fantastic group'. Evidently, they were called the Peake Family and they played fairy music. 'Al, it's incredible. See if you can find a record.' I found that they went into every eisteddfod and folk music concert around and had a really big reputation. They won every contest they entered. They would, in fact, be passing through London on the night of the party, so I asked the leader, who happened to be the grandfather of the family, to bring the group to the party. He agreed and I went and met him and set it all up. The Bonzo Dogs played and then I went on stage and received a massive barracking. I said, 'Please could you be quiet now because we're going to have some fairy music.'

I heard Paul go, 'Oh my God.'

They were fantastic. The old man played Uillian pipes which are different from bagpipes because you press a pad on your knee and they make this wonderful haunting sound. John Lennon went mad about the sound and I had to get him a set of pipes afterwards. There was a seven-year waiting list but with a bit of bribery and corruption I managed to get a set for him in about three months. 'I'll learn how to play them, Al,' he said. 'Don't you worry.'

I thought *Magical Mystery Tour* was great, and years ahead of its time. Unfortunately, the critics thought exactly the opposite. There were also an awful lot of private jokes that baffled the public.

Perhaps my proudest claim to fame from all my years with the Beatles is that I am the co-writer of the number-one hit Lennon and McCartney song, 'Hello, Goodbye' – even though I never get any credit for it.

Shortly after he split from Jane, I was up at Paul's house one night and there were just the two of us. He'd call me up for a chat and we would hit the scotch and Coke together. Not too hard, you understand, just hard enough to make us relax a little. We never got drunk, just mellow. I was idly marvelling at his gift for song-writing and he was dismissive. Paul said, 'Have you ever thought about writing a song? There is really nothing to it. It's dead easy, anyone can do it. Look, let's write a song together.' He marched me into the dining room where he had a wonderful old hand-carved wooden harmonium. It was a little organ and you had to pump to get the air into it with big pedals. He lifted the lid of this ancient instrument and said, 'Right, you get on that end and I'll be on this end.'

I think I was on the treble end and he was on the bass end. We both had to pedal like mad to get it going.

'Come and sit at the other end of the harmonium. You hit any note you like on the keyboard. Just hit it with both hands as you feel like and I'll do the same. Now whenever I shout out a word, you shout the opposite. That's all and I'll make up a tune. You watch, it'll make music.'

'Fire away,' I said nervously, feeling like someone suddenly asked to be co-pilot of an airliner. We got this rhythm going, just banging away on the keys. I think I had had just enough scotch and Coke to give me the confidence to join in.

'Black,' he started.

'White,' I replied.

'Yes.'

'No.'

'Good.'

'Bad.'

'Hello.'

'Goodbye.'

And so it went on for about five minutes until we ran out of pairs of opposites and went to freshen the drinks. A day or so later, Paul arrived in the office with a demo tape of 'Hello, Goodbye'. He said, 'Here's our new single.' I don't know whether it was already going round in his head or if he really did dream it up that night. A bit of both, I suspect. So those were the seeds of a Beatles number one, written, I will always believe, by Taylor and McCartney.

Another night I was walking with Paul from Abbey Road at around 3.00am after a long session. We were looking forward to a much-needed scotch and Coke at Paul's house. Two girl fans followed at a respectful distance. High up on the wall at the corner of Cavendish Avenue was an ancient lamp that looks like an old gas light. Paul stopped there and took hold of the acoustic guitar which hung round his neck by a piece of frayed string. He said, 'I've just written a new song. Would you like to hear it?' He took his guitar and positioned himself in the small cone of light from the lamp and sang this haunting song about a blackbird with a broken wing. It was a lovely still night and just listening to my talented friend singing this beautiful song made me glad to be alive. The two young fans stood back, eternally grateful that their long vigil had brought them such an entertaining reward. Later Paul played me the demo of 'Blackbird' and I was terribly disappointed that he had used all sorts of gimmicky production effects which for me spoiled the simplicity of the song he had sung that night. A second demo even had twittering bird noises added. Paul never could resist filling in any quiet holes in a song.

But at least John Lennon never sent me to prison, which was something Paul McCartney managed in the autumn of 1968. His song 'Ob-la-di, Ob-la-da' inspired Paul to call me up and say, 'I want you to get down to Brixton Prison with £800 in cash and give it to a bloke in there called Scott.'

Evidently, Scott was in prison for running up arrears over his wife's maintenance or some such civil debt, and more significantly, when not banged up he ran a band called the Obladi-Oblada band and he reckoned Paul had seen the flyposters and taken the name Obladi-Oblada off that. Apparently, he had got through to Paul about this strange, perceived injustice and Paul had said, 'OK, I didn't, but what are you after?' And Scott had replied that if Paul paid off his maintenance debts he would forget about the whole thing. So Muggins here, Mr Fixit, had to get £800 from nowhere on a Saturday morning and into Brixton nick. It was another case of over to you, you're Mr Fixit.

I called on a resourceful guy called Dennis O'Dell who worked for Apple as a film producer. He had done *Magical Mystery Tour* for us and he seemed the sort of street-wise individual who could lay his hands on a large amount of cash at short notice. He said, 'Bloody hell, I'll call you back.' When he did, he sent me to this second-hand car dealer in east London. 'Don't ask any questions, I'll sort out the repayment,' was Dennis's only advice. I expected the Kray Twins, but the guy I met wasn't that easy-going. He was a huge bloke with cauliflower ears and a bent nose. I just said 'Thank you' and off I went to Brixton Prison. There had just been a high-profile escape using a helicopter and all the security had been improved, which meant the nearest the taxi could take me was to some bollards 100 yards from the gate. I had to run through pouring rain and bang on the door to be let into the prison. After an interminable wait, I managed to pay, got the receipt and came out for another soaking on the way home. Working for the Beatles was definitely not all glamour.

If there was one Beatles romance that I thought would really last it was the love affair between Paul and Jane Asher. They did seem very much in love. I thought they were made for each other. Jane was just the most adorable woman you could expect to meet. She was bright and funny and incredibly attractive. I thought she was a wonderful match for Paul. And I think he thought so, too. She was well educated and very successful in her own right.

When it ended, it was awful. Jane came home to find Paul with Francie Schwartz, a groupie from New York. It was terrible for Jane. Francie was not just in the house but in the bed she shared with Paul. Jane was in a state of shock and her relationship with Paul ended there and then. There were fans waiting at the gate as usual and they tried to warn Paul that Jane was approaching. But Paul thought they were joking. He couldn't resist another woman.

Jane's mother came down later to remove all of Jane's belongings. I remember she also took all the household things that were Jane's. There was a set of pans she was particularly attached to. Paul stayed discreetly well out of the way.

Paul was absolutely devastated. Jane's departure shattered him. I have never quite been sure if it was because he really loved Jane or because he was so shocked that she had the nerve to turn down Paul McCartney. And let's not forget, they were engaged by now. She wasn't just his girlfriend, she was definitely going to be his wife. Afterwards, he had a succession of one-night stands, although often the relationship did not even last that long.

It's the only time I ever saw him totally distraught and lost for words. Normally he was so flip and cool and permanently full of confidence in himself. It was then that I realised how close we had become because I was the shoulder he cried on. We spent weeks together after the end of his love affair with Jane. It completely threw him. He pleaded with Jane to forgive him but she was implacable. She didn't want to know. She is a very strong and highly principled lady. I think she was deeply in love with Paul. And it wasn't just the Beatle stuff; she wasn't interested in fame or money. She loved Paul for himself. She loved his humour and his energy and she believed in him.

Paul literally cried on my shoulder. We hit the bottle together. Hard. He always seemed to feel lonely at night and the phone would go and Paul would say, 'Al, get a cab and come on up to Cavendish.' I didn't mind because he was a friend in pain. Yes, he was my boss in a way, I suppose, in that he was one of Brian's most important acts. But I thought the world of Paul. He was like the younger brother I'd never had. He was talented, charming and often very kind. I had watched his love for Jane grow from early infatuation into a deep and passionate love affair.

Paul told me how much he had learned from Jane and her talented family. He wasn't a yobbo before he met Jane, I'm not saying that. But he was relatively unsophisticated. Jane introduced him to fine wines, art, films and all aspects of culture. Jane's mother taught the oboe at the Royal College of Music. This was a whole new world for Paul and he loved it. He absorbed it like a sponge. Of course, being a bright bloke he was a very fast learner but I've always thought that a lot of Paul's taste comes from Jane. She taught him what good taste was.

That's why he found it so shocking when she dumped him. He went completely off the rails. He couldn't believe what he'd done and he couldn't have said that to any of the other three Beatles. Sure, musically they had become almost like one person and they were rock solid then in anything that threatened the Beatles. But individually they never liked to accept weakness. Paul would have hated John to think that he was upset about a woman, even if she was Jane Asher.

We would sit up at Cavendish Avenue until 3.00am and he would talk about what a prat he had been. 'I had everything and I threw it away,' he would say. 'Jane wasn't just my woman, she was my closest friend. I've told her everything inside me. She knows what makes me tick down to things that happened as a kid. I went right through all the stuff about my mother dying and how I dealt with that. With Jane, I could just relax completely and be myself and that seemed to be what she wanted. With the other women, I'm a fucking millionaire rock star who just happens to be about as shallow as a puddle.'

Other times he would just turn up late at night at my house. It would be midnight or 1.00am and Lesley and I would have long gone to bed. The doorbell would go and there would be Paul. 'Has Lesley got the kettle on?' he'd ask cheerfully, and I would know that I'd be up half the night going through how wonderful life had been with Jane. And he would put his arms round me and cry. Paul was never ashamed about crying. Afterwards, he'd try and crack a joke about it. 'I thought Jane was the drama queen, but it's me,' and he'd laugh weakly.

One night at Cavendish, Paul and I sat and drank scotch and Coke for so long that the first light of dawn started to appear as we were still putting the world to rights.

'Come on, Al,' said Paul. 'I need some fresh air. Let's take Martha for a walk.'

We were pretty relaxed but we weren't drunk. Martha leapt up from the rug by the fire and Paul and I piled into the DB6 and he drove us the half mile or so to the foot of

Primrose Hill. We left the car outside London Zoo and went through the fence up the hill. It was very muddy at the bottom and Paul looked at my footwear and laughed, 'So much for the man with the shiny shoes.'

We enjoyed the spectacular view in the first light of dawn. There was a real freshness in the air as Martha hurtled off in all directions in search of sheep or, better still, bones, and Paul and I enjoyed a few stolen moments of the day before the rest of London woke up. At 5.00am there was so little traffic noise that we could hear some early morning noises from the occupants of the zoo. It was chilly in the breeze that rustled the kites stuck up in the trees. Paul and I kept strolling around enjoying the experience and keeping warm.

'Look at that dawn,' said Paul in a whisper. 'How anybody can say that there is no such thing as God, or some power bigger than us. If you stand and look at that sky, you know there must be more to life than we can comprehend ...' We were totally absorbed in the sights and sounds of the universe in front of us, as if we were the only men in an abandoned city.

Then, suddenly behind us, a stranger appeared. He was a middle-aged man, very respectably dressed in a belted raincoat and he appeared to have come out of nowhere. One second Paul and I were alone, straining to see which direction Martha would come bounding back from, and the next, this man was there. He said, 'Good morning,' politely. 'My name is John.'

Paul said, 'Good morning. Mine's Paul. This is Alistair and that's Martha the dog,' as our four-legged friend returned swiftly.

John said, 'It's lovely to meet you. Isn't this wonderful?' and he walked away.

Paul and I looked at each other and I said, 'God, that was peculiar.' I looked round and there was no sign of the man. The stranger had completely disappeared from the top of the hill as if he had just vanished into thin air. There was nowhere for him to go, yet he had just evaporated. Paul and I both felt pretty spooked by this experience. We both thought something special had happened. We sat down rather shakily on the seat and Paul said, 'What the hell do you make of that? That's weird. He was here, wasn't he? We did speak to him?'

'Sure. He was here only seconds ago,' I said.

'Let's go home,' muttered Paul.

Back at Cavendish, we spent the rest of the morning talking about what we had seen and heard and felt. It sounds just like any acid tripper's fantasy to say they had a religious experience on Primrose Hill just before the morning rush hour, but neither of us had taken anything like that. Scotch and Coke was the only thing we had touched all night. We both felt afterwards that we had been through some sort of mystical experience, yet we didn't care to name, even to each other, what or who we had seen on that hilltop for those few brief seconds.

Paul tried to immerse himself in work. And then after some months he said, 'Do you know any birds?' I knew a young girl who worked in a bar and I asked her if she'd like to meet Paul McCartney. She certainly did and we went over to Cavendish Avenue together. But Paul just wanted to talk and he wasn't interested in sex that night. I put her in a taxi home before I left. Paul just wanted some natural

221

contact with someone female. He wanted a woman to talk to.

Months later, Paul rolled up outside our flat in Montagu Place on a Sunday morning in his two-seater Aston Martin.

'Come on, we're off to look at a house,' said Paul. But he already had Francie Schwartz and Martha as passengers. I said there was no room but Paul insisted and Lesley and I somehow got in and we all squeezed up and with him at the wheel we headed off for Kent. When we reached the grounds, Francie and Paul disappeared for about 20 minutes. We had to draw our own conclusions about what they were up to, but I'm pretty sure they weren't playing Scrabble.

The tour of the house itself was pretty uneventful, but on the way back down a dual carriageway, Paul suddenly slammed on the anchors and we screeched to a halt. He yelled, 'Did you see that?' as he executed an alarming U-turn. 'There's a village called Bean down here according to that signpost. We've got to go there. Then I can say I've been to Bean.'

Well, he's the imaginative songwriter; I just wanted to get home. But when we got there we could see that the most exciting thing about Bean was its name. It was the dullest village on earth. But it had a big pub and the doors were just opening. 'Let's have a drink,' said Paul, so we all trooped in.

There was no one else there, but the expression on the landlady's face said that she was well aware of who had just walked in. Before you could say 'Gin and tonic' her whole family was standing in a line behind the bar. They were clearly in awe and they were even more delighted when Paul decided to have a bash on a drum kit. Paul always fancied himself as a drummer so he did a quick solo and we finished our drinks and left with the landlady's mouth still wide open. They were fun times. Paul loved to blast in and out of people's lives in double-quick time. Whatever he said about the agonies of Beatlemania, Paul never really stopped loving the fame.

That appears critical and it's not really meant to, because he could also be refreshingly down to earth. Once, Lesley's mother and stepfather were staying with us for a few days. The doorbell went at 10.00pm and there was Paul with his usual question, 'Has Lesley got the kettle on?' Paul came in and my in-laws just sat there as Paul casually walked in and said, 'Hey-up, how are you?' I introduced them. For a moment, my in-laws froze in the presence of a living legend. He just flopped down and joined us. Afterwards they said, 'But he's normal, he's just like us.'

It was a treasured moment and no one can take that away from me. Another came very late at night at Abbey Road. It was around 2–3.00am and I was very tired. The boys had taken a break and I went looking for Paul to see if there was anything else he needed before I went home. I found him on his own in Studio 1, sitting at the big white grand piano and picking out this melody virtually with one finger. At first I just heard a few notes but I was instantly enraptured and, as Paul looked up, I said, 'Hey fella, that's great, what is it?'

Paul said, 'It's just an idea I've been playing around with.'

I stood and listened and it just got to me. I said, 'You must work on that melody line. I know someone who would absolutely love it.'

'Who's that?' said Paul, only half-listening.

'Lesley,' I said. 'She loves those pure and simple haunting lines.'

He smiled and carried on picking it out. There was a guy behind the control panel who had just been taping a demo for a song Paul had written for Marianne Faithfull that she never recorded. Paul raised his voice and called up to the guy, 'Have you any tape left?'

'Yeah,' came the reply.

'Roll it,' said Paul. And he began to play this fabulous song. I was totally transfixed. It was a very early version of 'The Long and Winding Road' and in terms of lyrics he hadn't got an awful lot further than the title, but when he started playing it I knew Lesley would love it. He filled in the lyrics with lots of la-la-las but it didn't matter. When he got to the end I stood and applauded. I said, 'That's beautiful, mate.' And I meant it; at moments like that, I had the best job in the world. I couldn't carry a tune in a bucket but thanks to Brian's advice and long experience I was starting to spot the real winners early on. And I've still never heard a song that makes the little hairs on the back on my neck stand up like 'The Long and Winding Road'. He checked with the sound engineer that we had got that and then said, 'Great. Now you get home, mate.'

The very next day, I was sitting at my desk arguing with a hotel manager who seemed unreasonably angry because his garden had been trampled upon by Beatles fans, when Paul arrived. He was wearing his long brown overcoat that he'd bought from Oxfam and he just went into his pocket and brought out this one-sided, white-labelled acetate which he handed to me. He just said, 'There you go, Al. That's for Lesley.' And he took out of his other pocket a 6in length of tape and asked for a pair of scissors. He said, 'This is the tape I got from EMI last night.' And he cut it up in front of me. He said, 'There you go, that is now the only copy in the world and it is not for you, it's for Lesley. I think we owe her a lot.'

We treasured that because I think it is one of those very rare occasions when one of the Beatles has been captured actually writing the songs. And do you know, I still prefer it to the finished version.

They were just four fun guys. They were four perfectly normal Liverpool guys who wanted to enjoy the experience of fame.

Cynthia Lennon is always seen as the typical Beatles' victim. But I have to say she never seemed like a victim to me. She was a funny, attractive lady who certainly put up with a lot of ill-treatment both mental and physical from John. But she was no bimbo. Cynthia was beautiful and intelligent in her own right.

The marriage ended badly for her in May 1968 when John installed this strange little Japanese woman in the house while she was away on holiday. Cynthia returned to find Yoko in her house with her husband. Yoko was even wearing her bath robe. The marriage ended virtually there and then and Cyn has been seen as the most tragic Beatle woman ever since.

It was never an easy marriage. John slept with hundreds of different women before, during and after his time with Cynthia. He had not wanted to get married in the first place but had gone along with it when Cynthia announced she was pregnant. During their time together, I often visited them at Kenwood, John's luxurious house in Weybridge, and it was a much more equal relationship than is ever portrayed in any of the numerous biographies. Certainly, Cynthia liked her sleep and used to go to bed early, which left John to go off into London and behave like any self-respecting rock star would.

But Cynthia was nothing like the clinging wifey that people who have never met the couple seem to imagine. And John was nothing like the rakish, thoughtless, faithless husband. Towards the end of the marriage, John began to suspect that Cynthia was being unfaithful. And like many adulterers he was absolutely frantic with rage at the thought of another man making love to his own wife. But because he was out all the time, and out of his mind much of the rest of the time, it was very hard for him to check up on what Cynthia was up to.

That is why he used his friend 'Magic' Alex Mardas to follow her. I don't think that Cynthia was unfaithful to John before he humiliatingly ended the marriage by moving Yoko into their home, but I know that John thought she was.

John quizzed me on a trip to Italy taken by Cynthia earlier in 1968. I hadn't arranged it, which was unusual but not unprecedented. Occasionally, one or other of the Beatles or their wives would take off on a trip they had organised themselves. But John thought Cynthia was being deliberately secretive about this Italian trip. He wouldn't tell me why he wanted to know, but he wanted to find out every detail of every conversation I'd had with Cynthia over the recent past. And such details were not the normal subject of John's interest. He was consumed by jealousy. He might not have loved Cynthia as passionately or as exclusively as he once had, but he sure as hell was not prepared to put up with her loving someone else. He had Alex spying on her and I think it was this obsessive jealousy that sparked him into bringing Yoko in and kicking Cynthia out.

Yoko received a lot of vilification because she broke one of the Beatles' unwritten rules. When they were working at Abbey Road, nobody went on the floor with them. Everyone kept out of the studio, even Brian and Neil, and certainly Jane, Maureen, Patti, whoever. We kept back when they were working. Unless they wanted us to hit something or bang something, which certainly happened from time to time. And suddenly this little Japanese lady is sitting at John's feet. You could almost see the other three shrinking backwards and thinking, Excuse me, we never do this.

That became one of the real reasons for the break-up. It was well on the cards before then, but it needed a final shove to force the boys into splitting and Yoko provided it. John knew what he was doing when he included Yoko in the inner circle of four. He was challenging the established order and saying that, of course, none of the other Beatles should bring a partner into the studio but John Lennon was different. He did not have to abide by anyone's rules. She actually took a bed into the studio at one point and the faces of the other three boys were a picture. If Brian had lived, he would have brought some order to this but he had sadly gone.

John was a bit of a lost soul until he met Yoko. If you looked at her and then at sexy Cynthia, you couldn't see why any man would exchange a beautiful, warm-hearted blonde who was the mother of his son for an oddball Japanese woman with more hang-ups than a psychiatric clinic. But she challenged John mentally. He told me once that she made him feel more alive than any person he'd ever met. I think because everyone treated her like a threat or a joke, he became extra defensive and she became more important to him than the Beatles.

When they decided to get married, I organised the flights. I flew over in the private jet to Paris and we parked up away from the main terminals. It was a beautiful misty morning and I saw John and Yoko, both in white, running towards the plane to meet me. I had laid on the champagne as always and they seemed so carefree and in love with each other that they ran over. We sat on the plane drinking champagne and I remember thinking that perhaps life was not so bad. It's a magical memory for me because they seemed so much in love.

In those days, there was a restriction on how much money you could take out of the country. I had smuggled some extra money for them wrapped in Lesley's tights down inside my trousers in a stocking. I think it was £500. I forgot all about the money in the emotion of the moment. I got off the plane and was waving goodbye. The jet started up, a little Hawker-Siddeley 125, a beautiful little machine, and I suddenly went, 'Oh my God, I've still got the money!' I had to stop the plane.

*   *   *

Paul's ability as a songwriter always mesmerised me. John could never be serious long enough to explain his creative processes. He said, 'It just happens,' as if he thought it was such a fragile talent that it might even disappear on too much examination.

But Paul was more open. I remember once sitting in Abbey Road's studio 2 with Mary Hopkin and Anne

Nightingale. The boys were there recording but they had stopped for a break and Paul had come over to where we were sitting by the piano. He sat down on the piano stool and we all chatted for a few minutes. The conversation turned to composing and Paul asked Mary, who had just recorded 'Those Were the Days' for Apple, 'Do you write songs?'

'Well,' said Mary nervously, 'the music is all right but I have trouble with the lyrics.'

'Oh but lyrics are dead easy. Lyrics are all around you,' said Paul. 'Let me show you.'

Paul turned to the piano and lifted the lid, inviting Mary to sit beside him. He played us the first song he had ever written, which was a three-chord number, then he showed how he had progressed to five chords and beyond that. 'Right,' he said. 'Let's write a song here and now. Let's think of a story – anything at all. Suppose there is a guy who waits every morning at the bus stop and there's this gorgeous girl who always stands next to him in the queue. But he is dead shy. He can't bring himself to talk to her, so he feels very frustrated.'

Paul picked out a tune and started to set the lyrics of the situation to it. We sat in silence, fearful of breaking the spell. 'Now one night in the darkness,' Paul went on, 'he goes out to post a letter at the letter box on the corner. Just as he is putting his hand up to the opening, the girl appears from the other side and does the same thing.' More lyrics and a stronger, more confident tune emerged. 'They both jump back in surprise, but they are both startled into talking to each other, which is a good job as she's as shy as he is. They fall in love and live happily ever after.' By this

229

time the song was virtually all there. There was a story and a melody and you could hum it. Paul went off to join the boys for a drink and Mary, Anne and I were left looking after him in amazement.

The boys all took an interest in Mary. One day, Mal Evans arrived carrying a shiny new guitar case. George had thought it was important for her to have a new guitar so he'd bought her a £400 Martinez guitar on a whim and sent it round. Mary was very moved. The only trouble was that the guitar was shiny as well and we had to put talcum powder on it when she appeared on television to stop the lights from reflecting so brightly.

But of all the boys, Paul had, and still has, the personality to charm the birds out of the trees if he wanted to use it. Paul has an amazing ability to make other people feel important. He has immense charisma and if he looks into your eyes and talks to you it's a remarkable experience. I believe his song writing ability is a gift. I don't believe he was a genius like John, but when he demonstrated his talent it was breath-taking.

Francie Schwartz didn't last very long, and a bewildering sequence of women processed through his life at that time. But Paul could be a very demanding boss. One weekend in the middle of a frantic recording session, Paul decided that he had to have a sunshine break. 'Get the jet and get me some sunshine,' demanded Paul. 'You decide where we go. There's my cousin and his girlfriend and me. Oh and I met this fabulous woman at the Peacock Club the other night. I want to bring her.' Only he couldn't recall either her name or her address. He just knew that she was a waitress at the Peacock. 'I want her to come. Find her.'

I found the club which was by then shut, but mercifully there was a guy there who knew which girl had caught Paul's eye – a Maggie McGivern – and he gave me her address. So I ended up walking to a flat in Chelsea where the young lady lived. I rang the doorbell and a woman's head poked out of a window far above me.

'What?' said a hungover voice.

'I wonder if you'd like to come away for the weekend with Paul McCartney to Sardinia,' I shouted up, hoping that not too many of Fleet Street's finest were within earshot. I'd decided on Sardinia while on my way to the flat.

'Who are you?' she shouted back. Fortunately, I managed to persuade her to come down and examine my credentials and she was then quick to accept the Beatle's offer.

I'd arranged flights from Luton in the private jet. In the car to the airport, Paul turned to me and asked where he was going.

'Sardinia,' I said. 'You'll love it.'

As they got on the plane, Paul said, 'Come on, Al. Come with us just for the ride. You can wait while they service the plane in Sardinia and come back with it in the morning. Then you can come back in it and pick us up on Monday. Come on, you know you'll enjoy it.'

I decided that a few hours in the sunshine sounded quite appealing so I made a quick call to Lesley and hopped on board.

After an hour or so of airborne champagne, the pilot let us know he was about to land but then we were all treated to a shock as the plane started to bank sharply and go round in what felt terrifyingly like ever decreasing circles. When the glasses started to slide of the tables I decided it was time to talk to the pilot. That is one of the advantages of hiring a private jet – you can go and ask the driver what is happening. The disadvantage is that sometimes you're better off not knowing.

The plane began its fifth circuit and I undid my seat belt and staggered down the gangway to the cabin. There I found the co-pilot looking down at the ground through the window beneath him. I tapped him on the shoulder and he removed his headset to talk to me. He explained angrily, 'The bloody Italians have forgotten to put the landing lights on. We can't see the bloody airstrip. You look out of the other side and see if you can spot it.'

Now I'm not normally a nervous flyer. But peering into the darkness of a mountainous island looking for somewhere to land does tend to concentrate your mind a little. At last the lights came miraculously into view and the pilot straightened the plane out and set us gently down on the tarmac. It was 4.00am and I was just happy to be alive.

A little later, having packed off Mr McCartney, his latest lady and assorted guests off in taxis, I was sitting dozing as the sun came up. The co-pilot tapped me on the shoulder and said, 'Come on, I'll show you why we didn't want to risk coming in without the landing lights on.' He took me round the aircraft hangar and there were two very large, very rugged mountains. 'We had to fly between those,' said the co-pilot. 'There's only about 60ft either side of the wingspan. It's a little to dangerous to risk without the lights on.'

Paul was more or less over Jane by then I think. He tried for a time to get back with her but messages were politely returned unopened and his calls weren't answered. The whole sorry finale to the Jane affair changed Paul McCartney in my opinion. For a few years, he had had just about everything he could ever have wanted. Jane was the first woman to reject him and he did not like the experience. Paul was a little harder, a little more cynical afterwards.

Linda Eastman set out to get Paul. Since her tragic death I've had the opportunity to reflect on my relationship with her. I can't deny that she made Paul a wonderful wife, to whom he was clearly absolutely devoted, and she was a fantastic mother to their children. She cared for Paul like no-one else, I have to be honest and say that we did not see eye-to-eye at all They met in the Bag O' Nails pub on an evening when the entertainment was being supplied by Georgie Fame and the Blue Flames. I remember him talking about a female photographer with really long and elegant fingers and he was smitten. Linda came with Heather, her daughter by a previous marriage. She was a charming kid and I used to bounce her on my knee many a time in those early days of their relationship. But I think Linda resented anyone who had been close to Paul, particularly during his period with Jane. It was very obvious at the start that Paul and I had a rapport that she could not quite come to terms with. She never stopped smiling but sometimes there was a glint in her eyes that I did not like. Paul and I had so many shared experiences that it was bound to be difficult for her. I tried to minimise it. I was genuinely happy to see Paul in another sensible relationship, and it also meant a lot less maudlin late-night drinking sessions that ended up going over the same old ground – Jane.

One of the first things Linda did at Cavendish when she managed to move in was to have the entire ground floor redecorated. Jane had decorated Cavendish Avenue in exquisite taste. Linda, however, wanted to remove every last trace of Jane from Paul's life. She didn't want to hear her name. She didn't want to see pictures Paul and Jane had chosen remaining around the place. It was like a new regime taking over and wanting to wipe the slate a completely clean. So in five days, the first thing I had to organise was the redecoration of the ground floor.

It was 4.00pm when the call came from Paul. Since Linda had appeared on the scene, our late-night chats had, not surprisingly, been terminated. But there seemed to be a change in Paul's whole demeanour at this time. He seemed cooler and as careful with his words and his warmth as he had always been with his money. I'd hardly seen the inside of Cavendish Avenue in weeks, so I was happy to answer the call. I had just arranged for Paul and Linda to go off on a five-day mini holiday and I knew they had to leave for the airport at 7.00pm so I knew I wasn't in for a long session. Paul answered the door himself and immediately said, 'Right, Alistair. I would like the whole of the ground floor of the house decorated by the time we come back.'

I was shocked and asked if he knew how long it would take to get a good decorator even if he was prepared to wait. But the way Paul had delivered his instructions left me in no doubt that he was serious and not inclined to discuss the matter. Behind him stood Linda with a small, cold smile on her face. And it was an expression which I was to see again.

Paul took me on a hurried tour of the lovely house, which looked exceptionally stylish thanks to the eye for elegance of Miss Jane Asher. Paul had a paint colour chart and I took careful notes as we went. Everything had been planned down to the last lick of paint and the last roll of wallpaper. The carpet in the huge drawing room was pulled up to reveal beautiful woodwork and Paul said, 'I want that polished and restored, but not to look like your ordinary G-Plan.' I knew exactly what he meant, but it was like receiving instructions from an impatient drill sergeant rather than a polite request from a man who had become a close friend. I had a feeling in the pit of my stomach, which told me I was not going to be nearly so close to James Paul McCartney for a while. Linda had decreed that the Indian restaurant flock wallpaper in the dining room was to go. The kitchen was to be stripped and the original wood exposed and varnished. The paintwork was all to be renewed and so on and so on until my head was reeling with all the details.

In the end, Paul tried to soften the changes with a flash of the famous smile that has charmed the world. He said, 'Now then, mate, when we get back I want it to be all done, and I don't want to see as much as a paintbrush in the house.'

The expression on my face betrayed my incredulity. I tried to suggest as much as I dared that he was asking the impossible, but he was not in the mood for negotiation. 'You can do it, Al. Never mind the cost. Just get it done.' I was dismissed.

As I left the house, I knew that our relationship had changed. My friend had turned back into my boss and I decided that, if that was the case, then I was going to be the most efficient employee imaginable. It was a formidable task.

Fortunately, a friend called John Lyndon put me on to a firm called Taverner's who were luckily based just down the road in St John's Wood. Ian Taverner listened to my request in deafening silence, right up until the moment when I said all this had to be completed in five days. Then he burst out laughing. 'It's absolutely impossible in the time you want,' he eventually recovered enough to say. 'Five weeks would be a better bet.' I pleaded that I really only had five days and begged him at least to meet me in the house and look at the job. He agreed to take a look at 8.00am the next morning, and after a sleepless night I showed Mr Taverner the scale of the job.

He said, 'What a great challenge. I'd love to have a crack at it.' I breathed a big sigh of relief but just to make sure he drew up detailed time sheets to organise the workload. It meant working through the nights with decorators operating a shift system but he reckoned he could definitely do it. And Ian Taverner was as good as his word. They didn't just decorate the rooms, they restored them. Every hairline crack in the plaster and woodwork was made good with filler, every trace of the old wallpaper was stripped off using a wonderful steam machine. Every surface was rubbed down and carefully prepared before it even saw a paint brush. On the fourth day, they even asked my permission to carry on up the stairs to the first floor, just to round off the job. And Paul's wooden floor shone like marble thanks to some superb workmanship. As the deadline approached, I was still nervous but at the appointed time, just six hours before Paul and Linda were due back, I went up to the house to find the foreman just leaving after completing his last checks. Inside, everything looked immaculate and there was only the very faintest whiff of paint in the air.

Paul seemed very perky when I saw him again so I put down his brusque manner before he'd left to pressure of work. He had certainly been in need of a holiday. He was delighted with the work and even Linda almost managed a thank-you.

I went up to the house with Ian Taverner's bill, which was actually for an awful lot less than I'd feared. Not that it mattered. Paul had told me not to worry about the cost. I showed the bill to Paul. He was sitting with Linda on the big sofa in front of the fire. Paul looked at it for a few seconds and said, 'Great. Get the cheque off to them, Alistair.' I relaxed for the first time in five days and was just about to put the bill back in my briefcase when Linda reached for it. I gave it to her. Well, she is Paul's girlfriend, I thought. She looked at it hard for about a minute and then accused Ian Taverner of overcharging Paul. Not only that, she looked at me as if I was something she had just stepped in and said, 'And how much are you making out of the deal?'

I was totally shocked. I could not trust myself to speak. My whole body seemed to go cold and shake with rage and my mouth was too dry to utter a word. I couldn't believe what she had just said. I just stood up, closed my briefcase and left the room. I can't ever remember feeling more angry or upset. Paul came after me and tried to act as peacemaker but in the heat of the moment I just didn't want to know.

'Linda's only looking out for me, Al,' he said. 'She's American. She doesn't know how far back we go. I'm sorry. Come back in and let's make friends.'

I didn't stop walking. I think in my mind I was walking out of my job as well as Paul's house. I was just so shocked that after all this time I could be accused of dishonesty by this hard-faced star-chaser from the United States. Paul was still speaking as I walked out of the house but I couldn't stop. If I had stayed there any longer I would have smacked him in the mouth. Or better still, her. That was the end of the intimate friendship between Paul and me and, as the car took me slowly back to the office, I thought I had better start looking for another job. I was just so angry because I had never even considered taking one penny that didn't belong to me. Paul, John, George and Ringo had my absolute loyalty and in years of spending millions of pounds on their hotels and flights and homes and countless other things, I had never taken anything for myself. Brian had inspired that sort of loyalty in people. He certainly did in me.

The following morning, Paul came into the office and tried to smooth things over. I smiled and said, 'Forget it,' but I knew I never could. Linda seemed worried about anyone who had been close to Paul. She saw them as a threat to her position. There may have been more singularly manipulative people around than Linda Eastman, but I've never met them. She might well have loved Paul but she sure as hell hated anyone who got in her way. I'd been his buddy through some of his recent unhappiness, so I'm pretty sure I was pretty high up on her hit-list. It only occurred to me much later that she didn't care in the least about the cost of painting a house. She just wanted to push away anyone who was close to precious Paul.

In the crazy Apple days, none of the relationships we'd had in the early '60s were the same. With Brian gone and

the boys struggling to see their future through an increasingly drug-induced haze, the abilities of even the famed Mr
Fixit seemed to be in less and less demand.

Paul did try to stay close and he did still need a reliable
fixer. He turned to me some months later when he wanted
to organise a facelift for his beloved Aston Martin DB6.
Paul loved to drive James Bond's car. It was a fabulous
motor and he came to me grumbling that he had been
ripped off by his garage after the latest service. Paul said,
'They call it a full service but nobody thinks to clean out the
ashtrays.' I knew what he meant. That was a typical
McCartney way of asking why the garage didn't restore the
car to its pristine showroom condition – and ashtrays
included.

I took the bait. 'Next time it needs a service let me organise it,' I sparked up. 'And I'll bring it back to you with more
than the ashtrays clean.' What a big mouth. Soon afterwards Paul presented me with his car and he said, 'Get me
a service done, then, Al. But not only that, I want it
resprayed. Get some colour cards and I'll pick the shade.
You get it done, fully serviced and resprayed and I want it
to come back as if it has just been driven out of the showroom.'

The garage came up trumps. They seemed delighted to
work on such a marvellous machine and the mechanic who
delivered the gleaming finished product back to Cavendish
Avenue was beaming with pride at the result. Paul and I
duly inspected the car. And they had done a wonderful job.
Fourteen coats of British Racing Green looked a treat and
there was not a speck of dust in the ashtrays. Paul walked
round it for ages lost in amazement and eventually eased

himself into the driver's seat absolutely thrilled. He looked like a kid at Christmas and I beamed back in all my reflected glory.

The bill was reasonable and Paul smiled his approval. But Linda strode out of the house to join us and my heart sank. A sense of déjà vu hit me like a flying housebrick. She snatched the bill from Paul, looked me straight in the eyes and asked, 'How much of this is going in your pocket?' This time Paul simply shrugged and looked away. I said, 'I'll see you then, Paul,' and walked away. There wasn't anything I could think of to say to her that wouldn't have made the situation about a million times worse.

Linda had no time for me. In my naïve and forgiving way, I don't think it was because of any innate character defect, but simply because I was part of the old guard and I was much, much too close to Paul.

SACKING
13

The popular view in our business is that pop stars who set out as ordinary decent people are corrupted into becoming grasping monsters by fame and fortune. That may be true of some band members or solo singers, but in my experience the Beatles were toughies from the start. That's not to say they couldn't be kind or funny or anything else if the mood took them. But when I first met them, they were already a tight unit determined to take on the world and get as much as they could out of it.

I was not just an employee. I was a friend. Of course, it was all because I worked for Brian but through that I thought came a good relationship. I've been to their homes and they have been to mine. I've worked through the night to make sure some flight or other was diverted to accommodate their travel plans. We were mates and suddenly, just like switching off the lights as you leave the room, it was over.

I had been pushing the Beatles to get someone in to sort out the mess that Apple had become. Money was draining from the company in all directions and no one seemed to be effectively dealing with it. I suggested that they got someone like Lord Beeching in. At the time, he was making himself famous for cutting back British Railways. I really was just using him as an example, but the next time I saw John he told me that he and Yoko had asked him to take over and he had turned the job down. I can't say I blamed him. By then, Apple was in a mess. The Beatles were drifting apart and I was already expecting the worst.

The American accountant, Allen Klein, took over. He had all the charm of a broken lavatory seat but he did have a reputation for being a ruthless businessman. I only ever once had a conversation with Mr Klein. I met him on the stairs one morning and I said, 'Good morning, Mr Klein.' And he grunted. It was not a lot to base your opinion on, I know, but could this curt, unshaven, overweight guy really be the new Brian Epstein? I thought not.

However I decided I could best serve the Beatles by keeping my head down and carrying on with my job. When the axe arrived I was in the Capri, one of my favourite restaurants, lunching with a man from Hawaii who wanted to book the Beatles for a farewell concert. He was offering $1 million, but it might as well have been $100 million. But he was a pleasant chap and he was also a top American football official. As the Beatles had a knack of demanding FA Cup Final tickets just as the teams were travelling down Wembley Way, I thought I would at least try to be prepared. My lunch partner cheerily agreed to let me have four tickets when Gerry the proprietor called me away to the telephone. I heard Peter Brown's voice and he did not sound happy.

'Can you come over to the office, right away, Alistair?' said Peter. I explained the delicacy of my negotiations but he was not interested. It was a crisis and I should return to the office now. When I got back to his office Peter Brown was sitting in his swivel chair and talking on the telephone to Ron Kass. In his hand was a piece of paper with a list of names on it.

'Yes, Ron, I'm afraid they are both sacked,' said Peter tersely. All of a sudden, the penny started to drop. I realised why I had been summoned. The expression on Peter's face confirmed my fears. I asked, 'Me as well?'

'Yes,' he answered. He handed me the list which had over a dozen names on it, all numbered, with mine at the top.

'When?' I asked.

'Today,' said Peter.

I was shocked, but I was not surprised. 'You are joking, aren't you?' I gasped as I struggled to come to terms with my life being turned upside-down.

'No, I'm not,' replied Peter sadly. 'Alistair, I wanted to tell you myself before one of Allen Klein's people told you.'

I tried to pull myself together and heard myself responding, 'Fair enough, Peter, but I'll tell you one thing. If I go today watch out for the bonfire where I'll be burning all the private papers and documents I keep for the boys in the safe box in my flat. I'm not coming back in here with them!'

'Oh, you wouldn't do that, would you?' he asked. 'Anyway the boys have said they want me to take special care of you.'

'What does that mean?' I said, starting to feel like a race-horse being put out to grass instead of being shot. 'Three months' salary and you keep the flat for three months, while you find something else,' he said.

The sheer unfairness of it all start to boil up in me. I was suffering from glandular fever brought on by overwork, and I'd booked to go to Ibiza on a trip to try to get over it. I snorted, 'I am not leaving today, Peter. I will come in tomorrow and clear up all my outstanding work. I will go, but I will go when I'm ready.'

I went back to my office to ring the boys. Not to plead for my job back but just to make sure that they knew what was going on. The whole philosophy of Apple was taking care of people, so I felt sure they would want information. I rang each of them: Paul, John, George and Ringo, in that order. And not one of them took my call. I got excuses from embarrassed wives and secretaries. I heard nervous Beatle voices in the background. But not one of my four famous friends came to the phone. And that hurt a hell of a lot more than getting the sack.

I walked round the building in a daze. Everywhere I went, I kept meeting other unfortunates who had just received their own bad news. Some of them were already clearing out their personal things. Others were staring hopelessly into space. Apple, the company that was going to put the fun back into the workplace, was under a cloud that day.

Like a man on automatic pilot, I somehow got through the rest of the day. I cleared my desk and wondered how on earth I was going to tell Lesley the news. We had some American friends coming round for dinner and I couldn't spoil the evening. Instead, I drank too much and put on an act to entertain them and said nothing at all about getting the sack. How I got through the meal I'll never really know, but I did and I went back to the office to do my final clearing up on the next day – Friday. I was determined not to leave anything undone.

When I got home, Lesley was in the bedroom sorting some clothes out in the big walk-in wardrobe. I said, 'Come here, love, I've got something to tell you.' She knew from the sombre tone exactly what I was going to tell her and said, 'I know. You've been fired.'

I said simply, 'Yeah.'

She put her head round the wardrobe door, 'In that case, we'll show them, won't we?'

That was when I broke down and burst into tears. She came to comfort me, sitting on the arm of the chair with her arm around me.

'Let it go, love. Don't bottle it up.'

I got the sack in 1969 and it still hurts. It's not the sacking. Obviously, if you give someone carte blanche to organise your business you have to accept their decisions. I understand that. But after all we had been through, for the Beatles not to even return my telephone calls was very difficult to accept. It sounds like whingeing, I know, but I was only the general manager of Apple anyway because John rang up and asked me to take over.

Neil Aspinall works for Apple full time now – he's the sole survivor, but he spends some of his time in court fighting to stop unauthorised use of material associated with the Beatles.

After being sacked, I tried to set up my own little management company. It was too late to go back to Robert Stigwood. That was another of my brilliant decisions in life. I found a little Welsh girl singer who appeared on Hughie Green's *Opportunity Knocks*, but I didn't have enough money to do it properly. I rang all sorts of people and nobody would really talk to me. They were all in a meeting. I found out later that they all thought I was earning a fortune so they thought they couldn't afford me.

Then I went to work for Dick James. He appointed me Press Officer for DJM Records and he put me in this room and said, 'I've got two young lads who are both very promising but listen to their stuff and tell me what you think. One was a guy called Sean Phillips, a very talented American boy, and the other one was this guy called Elton John. Well, to be honest, he was really called Reg Dwight, but both names were completely unknown in those days. I know it sounds glib and smug to say so, but he really bowled me over straight away. Not since I'd first heard the Beatles in The Cavern all those years ago had I heard such an original talent. Sean Phillips quickly moved back to America so I was left trying to get Reg or Elton into the papers. In those days it was very hard to get a break, even with the sort of ability Elton had. He and Bernie Taupin used to sit working together day after day and they were just desperate to make it.

Elton used to beg me to come to some of his gigs – he was only singing in pubs in those days – just to fill out the audience a little. He was that keen to get started, he even thought one or two more people would help swell the crowds. 'Bring the missus and bring some friends,' he'd say. Elton deserves all the success he's had since then, because he really worked hard. He wasn't proud. If I had any guests in the office, he was always happy enough to go and make the coffee without being asked.

My big idea was to advertise Elton on London buses. He had this wonderful album called *Skyline Pigeon* and I took advertising space on the back of 100 London buses. I thought it looked pretty dramatic but it was some time later before Elton John became a household name.

It was virtually hopeless trying to get publicity for unknown artists and I didn't seem to have any discernible gift for PR work. Dick only gave me the job out of kindness. But it wasn't working out and Dick and I had a friendly meeting and decided it was time for me to move on. I then worked for Saga Records with a guy called Marcel Rodd who I found too difficult to work for.

I saw a job advertised working for Morgan Grampian magazines as a project manager and I did that for a long time until Lesley and I spotted a chance to get out of London altogether running a craft centre and tea rooms in Derbyshire.

We saw an advert in the *Times* for a middle-aged couple to run this nice little profit-sharing business. We got the job and worked our fingers to the bone but it wasn't financially worthwhile.

We scraped enough money together to buy a house thanks to a loan from my father-in-law and I began a round of depressing labouring jobs. I've shovelled lead, made machine knives, washed pots in pubs. I'm not proud or very well qualified.

The Beatles were my life as a young man. I loved them all and I'm still trying not to be bitter about how I was treated in the end. I risked my marriage and I ruined my health. I was so determined to get the job done I wouldn't take a holiday, and I will always believe it is because of that that I contracted glandular fever, which laid me really low for a long time. But I still wouldn't have missed it for anything.

The Beatles took the piss out of the world for eight-and-a-half years. And when it stopped, I think a lot of fun went out of many people's lives. There is no question that as pop musicians, the Beatles were the best there has ever been, but as people it was difficult for them to live up to that accolade.